P9-DJA-690

FREE CASH FLOW AND SHAREHOLDER YIELD

FREE CASH FLOW AND SHAREHOLDER YIELD

New Priorities for the Global Investor

William W. Priest and Lindsay H. McClelland

John Wiley & Sons, Inc.

Published by John Wiley & Sons, Inc., Hoboken, New Jersey.
Published simultaneously in Canada.

For general information on our other products and services or for technical support, please contact our Customer Care Department within the United States at (800) 762-2974, outside the United States at (317) 572-3993 or fax (317) 572-4002.

Wiley also publishes its books in a variety of electronic formats. Some content that appears in print may not be available in electronic books. For more information about Wiley products, visit our web site at www.wiley.com.

Library of Congress Cataloging-in-Publication Data:
Priest, William W.
    Free cash flow and shareholder yield : new priorities for the global investor / William W. Priest and Lindsay H. McClelland.
        p.   cm.
    Includes bibliographical references and index.
    ISBN-13: 978-0-470-12833-6 (cloth)
    ISBN-10: 0-470-12833-X (cloth)
  1. Investments, Foreign.   2. Cash flow.   3. Portfolio management.   I. McClelland, Lindsay H., 1979- II. Title.
    HG4538.P686 2007
    332.67'3—dc22

                                                    2006036779

Custom ISBN-13 978-0-470-13000-1
Custom ISBN-10 0-470-13000-8

Printed in the United States of America.

10   9   8

CONTENTS

PART THREE

Strategies for the New Investment Landscape

FOREWORD

This book—*Free Cash Flow and Shareholder Yield*—must-read for individual investors, pension and mutual fund trustees, professional money managers, and anyone interested in the growth and preservation of wealth.

In this concise and very readable book, Priest and McClelland have put together a comprehensive analysis of the present equity market and the forces that determine its future value. Readers are rewarded with a method for analyzing market trends and an investment discipline designed to both protect wealth from turbulence and to profit from it.

The goal of successful investing is to take positions on assets that exhibit discrepancies between observed prices and fundamental values. Academic researchers call these discrepancies "market anomalies" and ask if they are real or a mirage produced by a lack of understanding of the forces that drive asset prices and their returns. True anomalies are those that the operation of market forces should remove in time. Trying to identify these true anomalies gave rise to the discipline of security analysis started in 1934 by Graham & Dodd's *Security Analysis*. Perhaps the main contribution of these pioneers was the introduction of discipline to security selection by providing guidance to the identification of hidden value.

Many things have changed since 1934. Accounting has become more complex and less informative. The capital markets have increased exponentially in size and variety of instruments traded, permitting levels of leverage impossible just a couple of decades ago. And the world economy and its capital markets have resumed their inexorable march toward integration as the impediments created by distance and lack of communication have disappeared in the Internet age.

It is at this juncture that Priest and McClelland's timely and important book comes in. The authors have identified the fundamental drivers of future cash flows and their pricing: globalization, rising interest rates, and deflating asset bubbles. Although these drivers are discussed daily in the press and by market analysts everywhere, Priest and McClelland go beyond their mere listing. They explain how they interact to affect equity values and use their analysis to develop a coherent investment discipline. How do they do that? First, they remove the veil from accounting earnings by relying on the present value of expected free cash flows. Second, they examine the forces at work that drive the future performance of the equity market. They observe that the growth of real global GDP and its distribution determines where free cash flows will be generated. Third, they explain how inflation and interest rates determine equity pricing. They examine the dynamics of housing prices, the role of liquidity and leverage, and the jump in corporate profits experienced in recent years and conclude that things are not going to be the same in the future. In fact, they note that the present equilibrium is already changing and that its displacement can be abrupt. Their analysis leads to the unavoidable conclusion that the bursting of the housing and credit market liquidity bubbles has just begun, and that corporate profit growth is unsustainable at its present rate. They also point out the increase in the cost of capital created by higher real interest rates and the increase of risk premia but they note that, although significant, those increases would not produce a collapse of asset values because of the present equilibrium between the political and economic needs of high-saving developing countries and a "dis-saving" United States. In a final instance, the effect of these changes on equity values seems to hinge on the balance between a slowdown in U.S. consumer spending and the incorporation of consumers from developing countries.

Priest and McClelland recommend scanning the global markets for the future sources of value to be found in companies that produce genuine free cash flow, not just reported earnings per share. They call this approach "Shareholder Yield": the ability to return cash to shareholders via dividends and share repurchases and to pay down debt. Shareholder Yield will produce excess returns as long as it is not fully priced by the market.

Throughout his distinguished career as an investment manager, Bill Priest has acquired a deep understanding of the interrelation between the stock market and the economy and its implications for successful investing. We are fortunate that he has put his thoughts and practice into writing. I firmly believe that, to confront the challenge posed by the extraordinary size of unfunded pension liabilities of the private and public sectors without a drastic reduction of our living standards, we need a fresh approach to investment management that goes beyond the exploitation of temporary excess liquidity. I believe that, in this book, Priest and McClelland show the way out of this predicament.

ENRIQUE R. ARZAC
Professor of Finance and Economics
Graduate School of Business
Columbia University, New York

PREFACE

As a veteran of the investment management industry, I have studied the stock market for over 40 years. In this time, I have seen numerous booms, busts, trends, bubbles, and phases. I have seen phenomenal growth and precipitous decline. I have seen the best and the worst of the global capital markets.

Long tenure on Wall Street has given me the perspective to place each of these market events—whether positive, negative, or neutral—into context. As an investment manager, it is my task to separate the passing fads from the paradigm shifts and to use these insights to generate returns for clients. I am writing this book because I feel that a true paradigm shift is underway in today's capital markets: one that will transform the drivers of investment returns.

Shareholder Yield is a term you'll be hearing a lot in the following pages. In addition to being the inspiration behind this book, Shareholder Yield is one of the philosophical cornerstones of my career as an investment manager and one of the founding principles of Epoch Investment Partners, a firm that my colleagues and I established in 2004. At its most basic level, Shareholder Yield represents a specific cash flow deployment methodology. But it also represents a different way of thinking about equity market performance.

There are forces at work in today's capital markets that will redefine how smart investments are made. Investors who want to protect and grow their capital will need to know why

the investment landscape is changing and how they can capi-
talize on the shifting components of equity market returns. I
believe that Shareholder Yield provides insights necessary to
answer these questions and offers the key to understanding
why the stock market's present, and its future, will be very
different than the last two decades of the twentieth century.

In an attempt to convey these ideas clearly and concisely,
this book is organized in the following manner. First, we assert
the importance of free cash flow as today's most meaningful
investment metric. Then, we present our argument for why the
order of the drivers of total equity return are changing and
what this means to the informed investor. We then expand this
idea to introduce the concept of Shareholder Yield: the notion
around which our book is based. This is followed by a discussion of several relevant events and themes in today's investment landscape, each of which can be tied back to the ideas of
Shareholder Yield and free cash flow. We conclude the book
by linking each of these concepts into a set of strategic recommendations that, when implemented through security selection
and portfolio construction, can both preserve and grow invested capital.

If my time on Wall Street has taught me anything, it's that
the rules of investing have changed before and that they will
certainly change again. Therefore, in writing this book, we have
been careful to approach the equity markets in a way that allows for change, yet also identifies what we believe are the enduring truths of investing. We have sought to highlight the
unique opportunities of today's marketplace by employing the
lasting and adaptable frameworks of free cash flow and Shareholder Yield. With any luck, this investment philosophy will
prove both flexible and robust, and will serve the informed investor today, tomorrow, and beyond.

ACKNOWLEDGMENTS

This book would not have been possible without the assistance and support of our colleagues at Epoch Investment Partners, Inc. and certain clients of the firm. We are particularly grateful to Genworth Financial Asset Management and CI Funds of Canada who supported our research and provided the seed funds for the execution of this strategy in the form of open end mutual funds (Epoch Global Equity Shareholder Yield and the CI Global High Dividend Advantage Fund).

We are also indebted to our manuscript readers Enrique Arzac, Emily Baker, Rob Brown, Doug Cliggott, and Mike Welhoelter, whose patience we tried and whose comments were invaluable in making this book a readable one. The expert assistance of Straightline was similarly indispensable, and we thank them for helping us create a polished manuscript. Our gratitude also goes out to Bill Falloon, Emilie Herman, Laura Walsh, and the rest of the team at Wiley for skillfully bringing this project to fruition.

Our research assistants were few but important. We want to thank Huma Bari, Rob Martin, and Jessica Wolf for their tireless ability to work with little notice and impossible deadlines. Without their efforts, we could not have completed our task. Special thanks go to Thomas Hu for providing an insightful and quantitatively rigorous approach to the free cash flow model, as reproduced in the Appendix.

Of course, all lapses, communication failures, and errors are our responsibility. We sincerely hope you enjoy the perspective we put forth in this book.

Wishing you a successful investment future,

W. W. P.
L. H. M.

FREE CASH FLOW AND SHAREHOLDER YIELD

PART ONE

Defining
Free Cash Flow and
Shareholder Yield

CHAPTER 1

Free Cash Flow

As a boy growing up in the 1950s, I was fascinated by the stock market. In the small Ohio town of my youth, my pals and I would cut lawns and trim hedges to earn spending money, but it seemed to me that the stock market provided an easier way to turn a profit. So, lured by the call of Wall Street, we devoured "How To" books on investing. Most of these books offered useless get-rich-quick schemes, variations of which can still be seen today on late night TV. There was no end to the bizarre trading techniques advocated by these authors; they touted stocks beginning with "x," ending with "x," stocks with no vowels. You name it, there was a book on it. In the more serious books, however, there was one variable that everyone seemed to agree on: That variable was *earnings*.

In the course of our studies, my friends and I learned everything we could about earnings and why they were endowed with the power to drive stock prices. We discovered that earnings represented the amount of revenues left over to the investor after all expenses were accounted for. If a company grew earnings, the company itself would become more valuable and this would be reflected in a higher share price. We also learned that, in order to arrive at a calculation of earnings, one needed

3

to follow the rules of accounting. At the time, accounting was seen as a sort of divining rod that properly separated assets from expenses, actual revenues from contingent revenues, and liabilities from real shareholder capital. In other words, there were few who questioned the concept of earnings or the accounting processes from which they were derived. And my friends and I were no exception.

Time passed, however, and my boyhood interest in the stock market developed into a career on Wall Street. In my very early days as a security analyst, earnings were still considered the most significant driver of stock prices. In fact, my first college textbook on the subject, *Security Analysis: Principles and Techniques* by Graham and Dodd (McGraw-Hill, 1962), centered its analysis almost completely on earnings. The discussion of cash flow was confined to 8 pages of a 723-page book!

As a result of this singular focus on earnings, most of us who studied or worked in the investment field during those years believed that the "fundamental analysis" of a company was all about the bottom line. However, in most MBA programs, there was a quiet revolution taking place that subsequently led to an explosion of novel ideas in finance that would turn the traditional earnings paradigm on its head. This revolution would not only change the investment industry as a whole, but would also completely transform my own approach to security selection.

This new financial outlook was based on the notion of *cash flow*. Specifically, there was a growing belief among investors and analysts that cash flow—not earnings—was the true determinant of investment value. In fact, the seeds of this idea had been sown several decades earlier when, in 1938, John Burr Williams's *The Theory of Investment Value* established the concept of "present value" in comparing investment opportunities. In doing so, he acknowledged the primacy of cash flow by describing "the investment value of a stock as the present worth of all dividends."[1] Now, a new generation of investors and analysts were expanding on Burr's ideas with the goal of developing fresh insights into the power of a cash flow-focused valuation methodology.

But these insights, however revolutionary, were not immediately embraced by the investment community. Because the cash flow philosophy flew in the face of those who continued to subscribe to the accounting/earnings paradigm, a gap was created between the traditional model of equity analysis and the model suggested by these new findings. For cash flow to gain widespread acceptance as a singularly valuable investment metric, it would take an event of great relevance to the investment community. It wasn't until 1984 that just such an event occurred: an event that would transform the common perceptions of what determines investment value and stock prices.

In 1984, a little-known private equity company called W.E.S.Ray (founded by Bill Simon, a former secretary of the U.S. Treasury, and Ray Chambers, an accountant) bought a company called Gibson Greeting Cards. Before being purchased by W.E.S.Ray, Gibson had already been the target of several acquirers. In 1964, Gibson had been acquired by CIT Financial Corporation, which was acquired in turn by RCA in 1980. Soon after its acquisition of CIT, however, RCA shifted its strategic focus to its collection of core businesses, which included names such as NBC, Hertz, and several high-profile electronics and communications companies. As a result, RCA decided to sell Gibson Greeting Cards, one of its noncore subsidiaries, to W.E.S.Ray Corporation for $81 million.

At the time, many observers on Wall Street thought W.E.S.Ray's purchase of Gibson was an ill-considered move. Even though Gibson was the third largest greeting card company in the United States with sales of $304 million, the company did not fit the model of what popular consensus deemed an exciting investment. Most of the investment community still adhered to the accounting methodology put forth by Graham and Dodd and, according to their earnings-based criteria, Gibson offered few indications of investment worthiness; there was nothing "flashy" about the company's financial composition, growth potential, or strategic capabilities. But to those who had discovered the value of the free cash flow philosophy, Bill Simon and Ray Chambers among them, Gibson could not have been a more attractive investment opportunity.

In Gibson, W.E.S.Ray discovered a set of characteristics that have since become the holy grail of every free cash flow pundit. Specifically, W.E.S.Ray found that Gibson possessed:

■ A stable revenue base that could take on a significant amount of leverage, and
■ The ability to consistently generate high levels of free cash flow that could cover the cost of the acquirer's debt and still allow the firm to grow.

With these characteristics in mind, W.E.S.Ray structured its acquisition of Gibson in the following manner: W.E.S.Ray gave Gibson management 20 percent of the company and, along with management, Simon and Chambers put $1 million toward the $81 million purchase price. The remaining $80 million was provided by various borrowings, including a $40 million loan from General Electric Credit Corporation and a $13 million loan from Barclays American Business Credit. To finance the rest of the purchase price, Gibson sold and then leased back its three major manufacturing and distribution facilities. Then, 18 months after the acquisition, W.E.S.Ray floated a public offering of 10 million Gibson shares at $27.50 per share. As a result of the cash generated by this offering, W.E.S.Ray realized a final payoff of $66 million on an investment of about two-thirds of a million dollars. In other words, W.E.S.Ray's return was nearly 100 times its initial equity investment. As for the

$80 million in debt, the newly public Gibson was now responsible for using its own free cash flow to repay these loans.

With the Gibson acquisition, Simon and Chambers had achieved something truly remarkable. In essence, they had acquired a company with the company's own assets, and then pocketed a fair portion of the proceeds when the company was taken public. Investors, especially those who had previously ignored the importance of free cash flow, could not help but take notice.

The key to W.E.S.Ray's success was its steadfast application of the cash flow model. Whereas traditional accounting metrics might have assigned Gibson to the dustbin, W.E.S.Ray understood that the company's solid cash flow characteristics made it an extremely worthwhile investment. By using Gibson's free cash generation to its advantage, W.E.S.Ray realized an incredible profit from an acquisition that no one else was smart enough to make.

The story of W.E.S.Ray and Gibson was important to me as an equity analyst and investment manager, and transformative for the investment community as a whole, because it brought to life the very concepts that had revolutionized and divided the field of academic finance decades earlier. Now, these concepts—which had all either asserted or implied the value of free cash flow-based investment metrics—had finally become practice. With W.E.S.Ray's acquisition of Gibson, financial insights crowded out the accounting models that had once held all but unquestioned sway over Wall Street. Instead of merely focusing on earnings, the Gibson story showed us that so much more was at stake in our evaluations of publicly traded companies. Cash flow, specifically, was the metric that would soon change the face of investing.

Today, there are few people in finance—or in any other vocation or field of study, for that matter—who would dispute the importance of cash. Entire civilizations, philosophies, and social orders have been created or destroyed with the goal of harnessing the power of cash. Capitalism, for example, is perhaps the most efficient process yet devised that allows both individuals and organizations to gain access to and control over cash and other forms of liquid capital. As the old cliché goes, cash is king.

Within the current investment landscape, cash—in the form of *free cash flow*—enjoys growing popularity as a key metric for investment managers, largely as a result of the lesson provided by W.E.S.Ray and Gibson Greeting Cards and the thousands of similar transactions that followed it. In terms of both security selection and the evaluation of business management, free cash flow provides the most meaningful gauge of a company's financial and operational health, and the most robust indication of share price performance.

We start this book with a discussion of free cash flow because of its essential place in the toolkit of the informed investor. But we are also using the concept of free cash flow as our jumping-off point because it is the cornerstone of this book's central investment thesis: Shareholder Yield. The rest of this chapter is dedicated to clarifying and expanding our definition of free cash flow with an eye toward the introduction of the Shareholder Yield philosophy.

Free Cash Flow—A Working Definition

In this book, the term *free cash flow* has very specific connotations that differentiate it from the more generalized concepts of "cash" and "cash flow."* Professor Enrique R. Arzac, in his

---

* We can also build a definition of free cash flow by aggregating the following components: cash dividends, stock repurchases, increase in the cash balance and marketable securities, debt reduction, and interest payments. With regard to capital expenditures, one can determine that acquisitions, reinvestment in capital projects, and expansionary investments net of disposals are needed to

book *Valuation for Mergers, Buyouts, and Restructuring,* presents the demarcations between these separate, yet related, ideas in the following manner:

> Why do we find it necessary to refer to a cash flow that is "free"? In practice, the term cash flow has many uses. For example, accountants define the cash flow of a company as the sum of net income plus depreciation and other non-cash items that are subtracted in computing net income. However, that cash flow is not available for distribution to investors when the firm plans to reinvest all or part of it to replace equipment and finance future growth. Free cash flow is the cash available for distribution to investors after all planned capital investments and taxes.[2]

A similar definition is provided by George Christy in *Free Cash Flow: A Two-Hour Primer for Management and the Board:* "Free Cash Flow = Revenues MINUS cash expenses PLUS non-revenue cash receipts PLUS or MINUS cash changes in working capital MINUS capital expenditures."[3] He goes on to say that the "'free' in free cash flow means that, after the company funds cash expenses and the changes in receivables, inventories, and fixed assets required to generate the revenues, the remaining cash flow is 'free' to be used for whatever management decides is best for the company."

In other words, free cash flow is a specialized concept that allows us to determine the true amount of cash available for immediate, discretionary, strategic use by a business. It is

---

support the production of free cash flows. However, managing capital expenditures to reduce those investments that do not meet the cost of capital will increase free cash flows. With regard to interest payments, they are excluded from this definition because they are not discretionary, even though they are technically part of the free cash flow assignable to both debt and equity investors.

important to note that the definition of free cash flow used in this book (and in the books by Arzac and Christy) is not the same as the concept of cash flow as determined under generally accepted accounting principles (GAAP) accounting. While the GAAP version of cash flow may attempt to arrive at a number that approximates a business' available cash, it is "nothing more than a reconciliation of the change in the balance of the 'Cash and Cash Equivalents' account to the changes in the other balance sheet accounts (and indirectly to the numbers in the income statement)." For investors, analysts, and managers, this is problematic because "both the GAAP balance sheet and income statement are riddled with accruals, some of which are disclosed and some of which are not disclosed." Free cash flow, however, avoids these unfortunate opacities because it "captures all cash flows in and out of the company, is not distorted by accrual items, and includes changes in working capital and capital investments."[4]

In the next section, we take a closer look at why traditional GAAP accounting is an inadequate investment and management tool, and why free cash flow provides a more effective way to gauge financial performance.

Free Cash Flow versus Earnings and the Price/Earnings Ratio—A Comparative Approach

The increasing importance and effectiveness of free cash flow is placed in particularly high relief when compared to other popular investment metrics—specifically, earnings and its derivative, the price/earnings ratio (P/E).

Why has cash flow eclipsed earnings and P/Es as the most useful benchmark for security selection and business management? Much of the answer lies in accounting: the process by which a company represents its financial composition.

Earnings, as defined by the accountant, are the residual of the application of GAAP applied to the recognition of "revenues" less related "costs." As such, earnings are intended to fairly represent the period-to-period performance of the company under review. However, over the past 20 years, GAAP standards have become less and less informative relative to the true financial health of a business. Although the GAAP system can certainly be credited for seeking to enforce a greater level of accountability and standardization within corporate financial reporting, the beneficial intentions of this process have become increasingly obfuscated. In fact, GAAP standards have grown so intricate and complex that their utilization is fraught with serious pitfalls for both management and investors. At over 10,000 pages long, GAAP is dense and convoluted and has resulted in the need for countless financial restatements and corrections.[5] As a result, the notion of earnings—resulting product of GAAP calculations—has become as ineffectual as the system from which it is derived. To put it in colloquial terms, accounting is like a bathing suit: it reveals a lot, but what it doesn't reveal is essential.

To better illustrate this point, let's turn to a well-known case study. In 1993, Jack Treynor, former editor of the *Financial Analysts Journal* and one of the truly great minds in finance, published *The Feathered Feast,* an investigation into how the concept of earnings can be a dangerously deceptive misrepresentation of a company's financial realities.[6] In this case study, a hapless portfolio manager for the Amalgamated Iceman's Pension Fund was lured into purchasing shares of Feathered Feast, Inc. (FF), a rapidly growing fast-food chain specializing in fried chicken. The investment in FF appeared to make a great deal of sense based on the past, present, and estimated earnings growth evident on the company's income statement. According to GAAP calculations, FF's earnings had grown by 10 percent per year from 1987 to 1990, and predictions of near-term future growth were said to be conservative at 12 percent. As a result, it came as a great surprise to investors when, in 1992, FF began to default on some of its lease contracts for retail sites. Soon, the company was unable to cover corporate overhead costs and resorted to auctioning off its assets for scrap metal.

In *The Feathered Feast,* the basic question posed by Treynor is this: How can a company with such exemplary earnings growth turn out to be such a remarkably poor investment? The answer, as it turns out, is not simply a function of the *idea* of earnings, but also the *process* by which this idea is formulated. And what, precisely, is this process? Once again, it's called accounting.

For our purposes, let's say that the world is divided into two types of individuals—the accountant and the investor. The accountant and the investor are at opposite ends of the financial valuation spectrum. The accountant has two objectives. The first is to fairly represent the state of the business at a point in time, which is done via the balance sheet. The second objective is to record the receipts and expenses to show profits or losses, which is done via the income statement. Conversely, the investor's objective is to use the accountant's data and the principles of finance to create a fair market value for a company. The investor does this by discounting future expected cash flows with an assumed appropriate discount rate. At the heart of the investor's assumption is the expected stream of cash flows to be derived from the net assets owned by the entity.

In other words, the investor is focused on cash flows while the accountant is focused on earnings. Because of this, the accountant is vulnerable to the many pitfalls and distortions caused by the presence of misleading accrual items within GAAP-derived financial statements. In the case of the Feathered Feast, the most misleading of these accruals took the form of depreciation.

Depreciation, in the eyes of the accountant, is represented by an annual charge against an asset's purchase price in order to reflect the decline in the value of that asset. The shortcomings of this method become clear when we realize how much variation and subjectivity are involved in judging how quickly or slowly an asset's value will decline.

Airplanes, for instance, are assets that were once commonly thought to have "useful" lives of 10 to 15 years per accounting conventions. However, after 40 years, many airplanes are still flying. Energy pipelines are another good example. There is an annual depreciation charge to the expected life of a pipeline, but do we really believe this pipeline is worth less on an annual basis when astute buyers are actually paying more and more for each additional mile of pipeline every year? By the same token, what is implied when a manufacturing firm builds a new plant with an estimated life of 30 years only to learn a year later that the widgets it was to produce have become technologically obsolete? In this case, should not the depreciation rate be 100 percent?

In fact, the accountant's miscalculation of the fair value of assets is the key to solving the conundrum presented in *The Feathered Feast*. To arrive at FF's projected earnings, the accountant had to apply an assumed rate of depreciation: a process that, as demonstrated in the prior paragraph, is an inexact science at best. It is not surprising, therefore, that in Treynor's case study the accountant's analysis of the value of FF's assets was wildly inconsistent with the economic reality. This is because the changing value of the assets (FF's retail structures) did not match the assets' ability to generate earnings over time. On FF's income statement, accountants had depreciated FF's retail structures on a 12-year basis. However, these structures actually became obsolete in only 5 years. Therefore, with the hindsight of this accelerated depreciation, historical earnings growth for FF was actually *negative*. Put another way, FF shares

only appeared to be a good investment when the annual estimated depreciation charge (on a 12-year outlook) was low
enough to keep earnings in the black. But, as soon as accurate
depreciation numbers were available in hindsight (on a 5-year
outlook), the company's true financial weakness was revealed.
Tables 1.1 and 1.2 show the remarkable disparity between these
two different outcomes. Specifically, estimated net income
changes from a positive $85 million under the accountant's ap-
proach (Table 1.1) to a negative $82 million under the investor's
approach (Table 1.2).

In light of this miscalculation on the part of the accounting
model, is it possible to trust the concept of earnings or the accounting methodology from which earnings are derived? Sadly,
the answer is no.

Thankfully, finance—the methodology employed by investors—offers an alternative, and more realistic, concept of an
asset's value and longevity. This concept is based on the present value principle, as first asserted by John Burr Williams.
This principle says that there is a stream of benefits (cash
flows) derived from the purchase of an asset, and the asset's

TABLE 1.1   Foresight Depreciation and Profit Analysis for Feathered Feast
($ in millions)

	1987	1988	1989	1990	1991 (est.)
Net income (after taxes)	58	64	71	78	85
Net income plus depreciation	100	110	121	133	146
Dividends	50	55	60	67	73
Capital investment	—	50	55	60	67
Gross plant	500	550	605	665	732
Dividends/Net income	0.86	0.86	0.85	0.86	0.86

Source: Financial Analysts Journal.

TABLE 1.2   Hindsight Depreciation and Profit Analysis for Feathered Feast
($ in millions)

	1987	1988	1989	1990	1991 (est.)
Gross plant	500	550	605	665	732
New investment	—	50	55	60	67
Restated depreciation	100	112	131	161	228
Net plant	400	338	262	161	0
Net income (after taxes plus depreciation)	100	110	121	133	146
Depreciation	100	112	131	161	228
Net income	0	(2)	(10)	(28)	(82)

Source: Financial Analysts Journal.

present value is determined by discounting this value by the firm's cost of capital.

To illustrate the difference between these two approaches to asset valuation, let's return to the airplane example. Recall that, under the accountant's approach, an airplane has a fixed life. However, under the investor's approach, the useful life of the airplane can vary greatly and, in some cases, be nearly infinite. Needless to say, these two approaches can result in wildly different values for the exact same company asset.

This is the reason the concept of earnings and, by extension, the concept of book value are often worthless tools for investors. Earnings and book value reflect the accountant's flawed concept of depreciation, as well as various other questionable accruals, and generally bear no relation to the true time value of the cash flows generated by an asset as reflected in the public securities markets.

Furthermore, there is no cost of capital within the accountant's methodology, even though cost of capital is incredibly relevant to finance. Why are investors correct in incorporating cost of capital into their calculations? Because the annual depreciation of an asset should not be immune to changes in interest rates, nor should depreciation be the same in an 8 percent interest rate environment as in a 4 percent interest rate environment. Simply put, the accounting approach ignores these critical details, while the finance approach incorporates them via the use of cash flow and the cost of capital.

From this discussion, we see that accounting clings to a method of asset valuation that is largely based on subjective and often quantitatively unsupportable assumptions. Therefore, it is clear that, for this and a host of other reasons, the concept of earnings is an accounting construction that is often of little use to investors and finance professionals. By extension, through the transference of the annual income number to retained earnings, the concept of book value (BV) is similarly erroneous.

If we follow this logic, it becomes clear that the popular valuation ratios derived from these accounting concepts—P/E and price to book value (P/BV)—also serve a questionable purpose. At the most basic level, P/E and P/BV are ineffective metrics for the simple fact of their flawed denominators. However, these ratios are additionally misleading because they attempt to combine accounting and finance: two philosophies that, as we have already learned, subscribe to radically different and fundamentally unblendable valuation methodologies.

A security's price reflects a concept based in finance (the present value of future streams of cash flows), while the concepts of earnings and book value are the products of accounting theory. To illustrate the dangers of mixing finance (a security's price) with accounting (earnings and book value), one need only refer back to the *Feathered Feast*. Before its collapse in 1992, FF stock had a remarkably high P/E ratio of 40, which seemed to indicate a level of confidence about its growth prospects and its investment worthiness. As we now know, this indication proved false and it is easy to see how the weak conceptual underpinnings of the P/E ratio are to blame.

For another example of why P/E and P/BV are not effective or accurate metrics, consider what happens when a company repurchases its stock at a price above its book value per share. The accounting treatment for this repurchase would result in a debit to Treasury stock and a credit to cash on the company's books. Treasury stock is a reduction from stockholders equity, so this transaction has the effect of lowering the firm's book value and therefore increasing its P/BV ratio, assuming no change in the market price of the company's public stock. It also has the effect of raising its "Return on Equity," because the numerator (earnings) has remained unchanged while shareholder equity has been reduced.

This situation becomes problematic when we recognize that some investment industry consultants use P/E and P/BV ratios as the sole means of differentiating "value" companies from "growth" companies. Value companies are defined as such because they have low P/Es and low P/BVs, whereas growth companies have high P/Es and high P/BVs. In reality, however, the actual characteristics of value and growth more often than not have nothing to do with these artificial descriptions. For example, from the previous discussion of what happens to P/E and P/BV during a share repurchase scenario, it is clear that a company could switch from the value category to the growth category by sheer virtue of the frequency and magnitude of its share buyback program. In other words, a "value" company could become a "growth" company, and vice versa, not through a fundamental change in the company's financial or operational characteristics, but rather through a mere reshuffling of its assets and shareholders equity components.

The main point of the past several pages is that accounting is a contrived language that often provides misleading criteria for investment decisions and investment style categorizations.

Accounting-related concepts such as earnings and P/E communicate little to an investor about the true profitability of the business, let alone a proper valuation for it. However, we can look to finance to provide superior insight into the true characteristics of an investment opportunity. This superior insight takes the form of free cash flow and its various applications.

Today, there are myriad examples of the manner in which the investment community has adopted the finance-derived concept of free cash flow as the gold standard for capital allocations. It is the rare Wall Street research report these days that does not mention cash flow and the valuation metrics that incorporate it. In addition, leveraged buyout (LBO) firms and private equity (PE) funds focus almost exclusively on cash flow as the measure of value creation. Because so many of these LBO/PE acquisitions involve placing a great deal of debt on the target company's books, the target company must be able to generate the cash flow necessary to service this new debt and to allow the acquirers to realize a profit. (Recall the example of Gibson Greeting Cards from earlier in the chapter.) For this reason, LBO and PE investors use a free cash flow model when evaluating takeover prospects. The success of this strategy is underscored when we consider that, in 2005, the net amount of capital raised by global private equity funds was $272 billion, nearly double the level from the prior year.[7] As of September 2006, this number increased to over $400 billion. In our view, this evidence of the growing popularity of private equity investing also indicates the heightened relevance of the cash flow metrics these funds are known to employ.

There are also many recent books and articles that support the use of free cash flow benchmarks for both investors and managers. Two of these books stand out in particular, both of which have already been cited in this chapter. *Free Cash Flow*, by George Christy is an excellent synopsis of how and why management teams should use the free cash flow model to create shareholder value. In Christy's words: "maximizing free cash flow maximizes a company's options and opportunities."[8]

The second book is *Valuation for Mergers, Buyouts, and Restructuring* by Enrique Arzac. Arzac, a professor of Finance at Columbia University's Graduate School of Business, provides an in-depth examination of the complexities involved in determining valuations for business units that generate cash flow. This book demystifies the entire subject of valuation and provides a level of granularity uncommon to most textbooks on this topic. At the core of Arzac's argument is the notion that— in the game of mergers and acquisitions, restructurings and common share ownerships—buyers pay for cash flow, not earnings.

In addition, both Arzac and Christy point out that GAAP accounting, the process by which earnings are derived, was never intended to be a management tool. Instead of GAAP, free cash flow metrics should be used to evaluate performance. Free cash flow offers a superior method because it incorporates the company's entire value chain (revenues, margins, working capital requirements, and capital expenditures) into one formula. In presenting this argument, Arzac and Christy align themselves with the pioneers of the free cash flow philosophy, which concluded long ago that a company's stock price is determined by the stock market's assessment of the firm's expected cash flows, not its historical earnings or GAAP earnings.

It seems clear that the investment community has already begun to embrace the idea of free cash flow as the stock market's most compelling and effective valuation benchmark. Similarly, we believe that investors and managers are ready to jettison the outdated system of traditional management accounting principles in favor of the superior insights offered by finance-derived cash flow metrics. The next section begins to specify the manner in which these metrics can be employed by the investment community within the framework of Shareholder Yield.

The Five Possible Uses of Free Cash Flow— An Introduction to Shareholder Yield

In addition to being the most useful metric for investors, free cash flow is also the metric that enables a company's management team to review and select the best possible options for the generation of shareholder value in light of the firm's cost of capital. Therefore, when engaged in the process of security selection, it is necessary for investors to look not only at the quantity and quality of a company's free cash flow, but also the manner in which this free cash flow is deployed by management.

From the perspective of a company's management team, there are only five possible uses of free cash flow:

1. Cash dividends
2. Stock repurchases
3. Debt reduction
4. Acquisitions
5. Reinvestment in company capital projects

Every conceivable option for the allocation of a dollar of free cash flow use falls into one of these five applications. Often, management will employ some of each, but we see a distinction between the first three uses and the latter two. We believe that, unless the return on incremental capital is superior to the firm's average cost of capital, there is little point in pursuing option 4 (making acquisitions) or option 5 (reinvesting in the business beyond maintenance capital expenditures).

So, when and if acquisitions and reinvestments fail to generate sufficient returns, free cash flow should be returned to shareholders via one of the first three options. These first three possible uses of free cash flow (cash dividends, stock repurchases, and debt reduction) are all effectively dividends payable to shareholders. Therefore, we refer to these three options collectively as Shareholder Yield.

The concept of Shareholder Yield plays a key role in the pages that follow. As we move on to a more comprehensive analysis of these three cash flow deployment options, it is our hope that this first chapter has set the stage for the discussion that will follow. So far, we have endeavored to use the "accounting versus finance" dichotomy to explain why P/Es (the products of accounting) are out and free cash flows (the products of finance) are in. Similarly, we have used free cash flow to derive the components of Shareholder Yield: a concept that is not only crucial to our investment framework but absolutely necessary for informed stock selection. In the next chapter, we explore the notion of Shareholder Yield more fully in order to further strengthen the case for this application of the free cash flow deployment philosophy.

CHAPTER 2

The Sources of Equity Return

In Chapter 2, we broaden and deepen our discussion of Shareholder Yield. First, we discuss the motivations for and the effects of employing each of the three cash flow deployment options from which it is comprised. Second, we link the concept of Shareholder Yield to the past, present, and future performance of the equity markets. Third, we take a larger view of historical stock market performance in order to define the various components of total equity returns. Finally, we revisit the role of the price/earning (P/E) ratio and set the stage for an in-depth discussion of the ratio's decreasing contribution to total equity market returns.

At its essence, the goal of Chapter 2 is to make Shareholder Yield a concrete and meaningful tool for the informed investor. By further defining its three components and by placing it in a historical context, we hope to show its ascending prominence within today's investment landscape.

The Components of Shareholder Yield—Three Options, One Strategy

As discussed in Chapter 1, the term *Shareholder Yield* is essentially shorthand for a three-part, dividend-oriented approach to free cash flow deployment.

The three components of Shareholder Yield are:

1. Cash dividends
2. Stock repurchases
3. Debt reduction

We have grouped these three cash flow deployment options together into one overall concept because they are all strategies by which a company can enhance shareholder value. In other words, each of these three uses of free cash flow has the potential to positively affect the return on a shareholder's investment. Therefore, they can all be seen as different ways in which to create a dividend.

The first cash flow deployment option on our list—the cash dividend—is perhaps the most obvious way of creating shareholder return in the manner just described.

The second option—stock repurchase—is also a clear method for value creation. However, a stock buyback will only boost shareholder return when the shares are cancelled or held in treasury but *not* used as a device to make up for dilution from option issuances to management and others.

Finally, debt reduction can also be used to create shareholder value and, therefore, to produce a de facto dividend. To understand why this is the case, it is helpful to consider the famous finance paper by Franco Modigliani and Merton Miller.[1] These two Nobel laureates proved that a firm's value is independent of how it is financed, provided that one ignores the tax effect of debt interest. If Modigliani and Miller are correct, the use of free cash flow to repay debt results in a wealth transfer from the debtor to the shareholder. Since the value of the firm remains the same, shareholder wealth is increased as debt is reduced. And this, according to our methodology, can be considered a type of dividend.

The ability to provide a return to the shareholder (i.e., a dividend) is therefore the uniting factor that joins cash dividends, share repurchases, and debt reduction under the conceptual umbrella of Shareholder Yield. But before we continue our discussion of Shareholder Yield and its role in today's stock market, we should first revisit the other two uses of cash flow that are not included in our definition of this concept: acquisitions and reinvestment. It is important to remember that acquisitions and reinvestment are perfectly viable, and often very desirable, ways to deploy free cash flow. However, to use cash in these ways, a company must follow the rules. As mentioned earlier in Chapter 1, the rules state that acquisitions and reinvestments should only be undertaken when the return on incremental capital is superior to the firm's average cost of capital. If this is not the case, the three cash flow deployment options comprising Shareholder Yield should be utilized instead.

A good way to think about this is by grouping acquisitions and reinvestments into a concept called *Firm Growth,* as opposed to Shareholder Yield. Firm Growth can be thought of as a growth concept, whereas Shareholder Yield is a value concept in the sense that, when this strategy is utilized, excess capital in the firm is returned to the shareholders. Apple Computer provides a current example of a growth company that has been deploying free cash flow via Firm Growth as opposed to Shareholder Yield. For Apple, it has paid for the company to use its cash flow for internal reinvestment in R&D projects. In this way, Apple has been able to generate the innovations necessary to maintain a rising return on the capital employed within the business. Other companies in other industries, however, will not realize such a dramatic pay off from reinvestment or acquisitions. For these companies, cash flow should be utilized according to the three components of Shareholder Yield. The lodging industry includes several companies such as Marriott, Starwood, and Intercontinental that have exhibited a historical tendency toward cash deployment in the form of dividends, share buybacks, and debt paydowns. While each of these companies has also invested in the development of new hotel formats or expansion into new geographies, they have not used all their cash in this manner because of the heightened costs of acquiring and building new properties within the hotel industry. As a result, Marriott, Starwood, and Intercontinental have elected to return a meaningful portion of their cash flow to shareholders, rather than spend it through acquisitions or reinvestment. In fact, over the past five years, these companies have channeled approximately $18.6 billion into cash dividends, share buybacks, and debt paydowns, thereby illustrating their awareness of the Shareholder Yield philosophy.

The Three Drivers of Equity Market Performance

Now that we have explored the three components of Shareholder Yield, it is time to look at the larger picture of how this concept will play into the future performance of the equity markets. For investors, the question is this: How can an understanding of Shareholder Yield allow us to make better informed and more profitable investment decisions? The information provided in Figures 2.1 and 2.2 allows us to begin formulating an answer.

Figures 2.1 and 2.2 illustrate the rolling 10-year compound annual growth rates of equities as measured by the S&P 500. As the legend indicates, there are five elements to these charts, three of which are the actual drivers of stock market return: P/E Change, EPS Growth and Dividends. P/E Change refers to the amount of stock market growth or decline that has been driven specifically by P/E expansion or contraction. Similarly, these figures also show the amount of stock market return that has been driven by EPS Growth and Dividends, which also include dividend reinvestment. These three drivers serve as a catch-all for any dynamic within the marketplace that results in a change to stock price, and any movement in aggregate equity return can be traced back to them. The calculation of total equity returns presented in these figures also includes a measurement of Combined Effects. This measurement does not represent a driver of returns. Rather, it represents the "compound" aspect of the "ten-year compound annual growth rates" displayed in these figures.*

---

*The following example shows why the Combined Effects value must be included in calculating the total return. Imagine we invest \$1 at time 0 (Value_0 = \$1) in a company, and its stock is quoted in terms of its P/E ratio. If our investment proves profitable, the stock's P/E may expand, and the value of our investment at the end of the holding period t may be:

$$\text{Value}_t = 1 + (\text{P/E Change})$$

However, to get the value in terms of the stock's actual price, we also need to consider the growth in earnings. This is necessary because, by quoting our investment in terms of the P/E multiple, we have implicitly discounted the EPS growth effect and that must be added back. Therefore, due to price appreciation, our value calculation expands to:

$$\text{Value}_t = (1 + \text{P/E Change}) \times (1 + \text{EPS Growth})$$

But there is more to it. As the company's earnings grow, the shareholders can also enjoy the return from dividend and dividend reinvestment. That further boosts our total value to:

$$\text{Value}_t = (1 + \text{P/E Change}) \times (1 + \text{EPS Growth}) \times (1 + \text{Dividends}).$$

The total return is therefore:

$$\frac{\text{Value}_t}{\text{Value}_0} - 1$$

For illustration purposes, Figures 2.1 and 2.2 show the return arithmetically linked (added) rather than geometrically linked (multiplied). The Combined Effects bar represents the difference between the geometrically linked and the arithmetically linked returns and can be attributed, in part, to each of the three component returns.

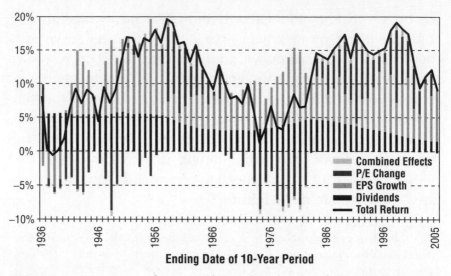

FIGURE 2.1   Components of Compound Annual Total Returns for Trailing 10-Year Periods (S&P 500 Composite, 1936–2005)

Source: Standard & Poor's.

Finally, the figures include a trend line that shows Total Return, the final sum of each of these interacting drivers.

Figures 2.1 and 2.2 present the same data points from two slightly different perspectives. Figure 2.1 breaks down the contribution made by each driver of returns for rolling 10-year periods beginning in 1936 and ending in 2005. Figure 2.2 displays the same data, but in a decade-by-decade format since 1927. There are seven and one half decades displayed, and Table 2.1 on page 30 shows the numerical breakdown of the data used in Figure 2.2.

What do these graphs have to do with our previous discussion of Shareholder Yield? To answer this question, first look at the historical role played by P/E ratios within total market return. In analyzing these graphs, we can see that double-digit returns occur when P/E ratios expand, and low to mid-single-digit returns occur when P/E multiples contract. In the periods of time when P/E multiples contract, earnings and dividends—the

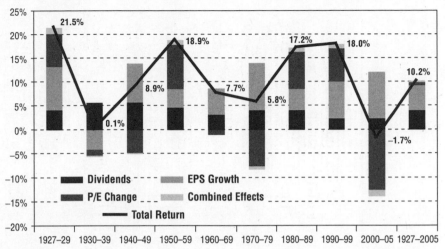

FIGURE 2.2   Components of Total Return by Decade (S&P 500 Index, 1927–2005)
Source: Standard & Poor's.

solid and shaded bars—acquire greater explanatory power in determining returns, as those two factors are almost always positive over rolling 10-year periods. Indeed, in some cases, increases in dividend yield and earnings per share explain more than 100 percent of the 10-year gains in the stock market.

In the next chapter, we will see how the market drivers of dividend yield and earnings per share are related to a Shareholder Yield-based approach to investing. First, however, it is necessary to address the topic of the P/E ratio and its effect on past, present, and future equity returns.

P/E Ratios and Interest Rates—Linking the Real and Financial Economies

Despite the consistent contribution of earnings and dividends, P/E variation appears to have the largest overall impact on valuation over the periods shown in Figures 2.1 and 2.2. Therefore,

TABLE 2.1 Components of Total Return by Decade (S&P 500 Index 1927–2005)

Decade	A EPS Growth (%)	B P/E Change (%)	C Price Appreciation (%)	D Dividends (%)	E Combined Effects (%)	F Total Return (%)
1927–1929	9.1	7.0	16.7	4.1	1.3	21.5
1930–1939	–4.1	–1.2	–5.3	5.7	–0.2	0.1
1940–1949	8.1	–4.8	3.0	5.7	–0.2	8.9
1950–1959	3.9	9.4	13.6	4.7	1.0	18.9
1960–1969	5.5	–1.0	4.4	3.1	0.1	7.7
1970–1979	9.9	–7.6	1.6	4.1	–0.7	5.8
1980–1989	4.4	7.8	12.6	4.1	0.9	17.2
1990–1999	7.7	7.1	15.3	2.3	0.9	18.0
2000–2005	9.8	–12.5	–4.0	2.4	–1.3	–1.7
1927–2005	5.2	0.6	5.9	4.0	0.3	10.2
Fraction of total return	51.5	6.2	58.0	39.6	2.7	100.0

Source: Standard & Poor's.

it is important to take a closer look at what affects the composition and movement of P/E ratios.

Over long periods of time, P/E ratios are largely determined by two interrelated factors: inflation and interest rates. To show why this is the case, let's take a look at the relationship between the "real economy" and the "financial economy." The real economy and the financial economy are essentially two sides of the same coin, so that the values of the capital markets (i.e., the financial economy) are linked to and driven by the events in the real economy. Figure 2.3, a well-known textbook model, reflects this linkage.

A connection between the real economy and the financial economy can be further established by looking at the historical values of nominal Gross Domestic Product (GDP; representative of the real economy) and EPS (representative of the financial economy). Figure 2.4 shows the remarkable correlation between the long-term growth of these two indicators.

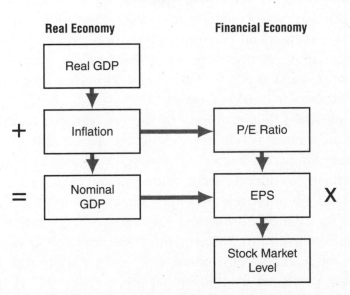

FIGURE 2.3   Linking the Real Economy and the Financial Economy

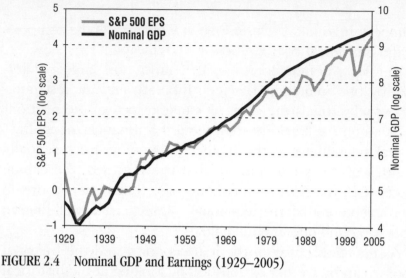

FIGURE 2.4   Nominal GDP and Earnings (1929–2005)
Source: Standard & Poor's, Federal Reserve.

As previously mentioned, the most volatile variable within the interlinking model of the real and financial economies is the P/E ratio. Whereas earnings almost always rise, P/E ratios fluctuate, rising in some years and falling in others. Why do these fluctuations occur? Because, according to our model of the real and financial economies, inflation expectations drive long-term interest rates, and long-term interest rates are the discounting mechanism for future cash flows/earnings and are therefore the driver of P/E ratios.

To illustrate the sensitivity of the P/E variable to inflation and interest rates, it has been estimated that a 50 basis point change in long-term interest rates roughly translates into a one point change in the S&P's fair value multiple. Put another way, a 200 basis point change in bond yields would trim about four points from the S&P's forward P/E versus that number in a 4 percent interest rate environment. This happens because, in higher interest rate environments, the cash earnings that a company produces in the future are worth less when discounted back at the present day's higher rates. With this degree of sensitivity, we can see how a rise in bond yields provides a headwind for equities unless overcome by earnings growth from a robust economy.

This close correlation between P/E ratios and interest rates can be seen in Figure 2.5. Specifically, P/E ratios are inversely correlated with interest rates—falling when rates rise, and rising when rates fall.

It is clear from Figure 2.5 that, since reaching a high over two decades ago, interest rates have recently shown an overall pattern of decline. Ten-year Treasury bond yields peaked at 15.8 percent in September 1981. Since then, interest rates have decreased steadily, bottoming at 3.11 percent on June 13, 2003. We have now entered a period of flat or rising rates. Today, for example, the 10-year U.S. Treasury is more than 150 basis points above the 3.11 percent low point. For the foreseeable future, it is reasonable to expect that interest rates are more

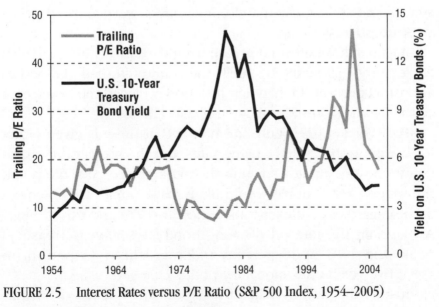

FIGURE 2.5   Interest Rates versus P/E Ratio (S&P 500 Index, 1954–2005)

Source: Standard & Poor's, Federal Reserve.

likely to rise than fall, which will place downward pressure on P/E ratios.

A Recent History of Interest Rates

To understand the consequences of today's environment of flat-to-rising rates, it will be helpful to gain some historical perspective on the matter. Prior to 2003, the last time interest rates bottomed was 1946, the year that Congress enacted the Full Employment Act of 1946. That Act required the government and the Federal Reserve to pursue three objectives: full employment, stable prices, and maximum growth consistent with a full-employment economy. Two out of three objectives—full employment and maximum growth—were realized. However, the specter of the 1930s, with its breadlines and homelessness, continued to plague economic policy makers, causing the goal of stable prices to fall by the wayside. As a result, the goals of growth and employment were allowed to supersede price stability.

As a result, interest rates rose irregularly from 1946 to 1981, for a total of 35 years. By 1981, the prime rate had climbed to almost 19 percent. Only when inflation replaced the bogeyman of the Depression did policy emphasis change.

Paul Volcker, the Fed Chairman at that time, is given credit for breaking the cycle of rising rates, but the seeds of its disintegration were already sown in the marketplace. At some point, the interest rate bubble would likely have burst of its own accord. Regardless, Volcker took action in 1979 and raised rates. As a result, the rate on the long bond (the 30-year Treasury) peaked in 1981 at 15 percent and was still at 13 percent in 1984, five years after monetary policy changed.

Just as the waning fear of inflation finally caused rates to retreat from the highs of 1981, concerns about deflation caused them to bottom out in 2003. The fear of deflation arose because of poor job growth, "economic output gaps,"* and the impending impact of hundreds of millions of low-paid workers from the emerging world (principally China and India) joining the global economy. Our country began to pursue monetary and fiscal policies with maximum vigor to prevent deflation. In a sense, the Full Employment Act of 1946 was turned on its head. Now, over half a century later, we had stable prices but not full employment or a level of GDP consistent with full employment (hence, the focus on "output gaps" within developed countries).

The effects of the expansionary policies in the first years of the new millennium are still very visible in today's U.S. economy, particularly in the form of the increased indebtedness that was made possible by several subsequent years of low interest rates. In 2005, total mortgage debt outstanding (which includes home, commercial, multifamily, and farm) exceeded $11 trillion, a 61 percent increase over 2001. Floating rate mortgage debt, which remains increasingly popular, has risen significantly as a proportion of total mortgage debt, providing further evidence of the effect of sustained low interest rates. In fact, according to *Inside Mortgage Finance,* an estimated $1.49 trillion of adjustable rate mortgages (ARMs) were originated in 2005, representing 48 percent of total mortgage originations. Furthermore, 32 percent of conventional single-family mortgage originations were for adjustable rate mortgages; counting interest-rate only ARMs, this percentage increases to more than 50 percent. In addition, consumer debt (largely credit card and auto debt) exceeded $2 trillion in 2005 ($2.35 trillion as of July 2006), over twice that of 10 years ago. Furthermore, total

---

*An "output gap" is the difference between the level of GDP and the amount of GDP theoretically possible if all available resources were being fully utilized (e.g., no unemployment, factory operating rates at capacity).

household debt has grown nearly 122 percent within the 1996 to 2005 period.[2] The estimated required payments on this household debt as a percentage of disposable income had risen to nearly 14 percent in 2005 versus 12 percent in 1996. If we reconsider this ratio in terms of total household debt as a percentage of disposable income, the number rises to a staggering 130 percent, as shown in Figure 2.6.

When we add to these consumer balance sheet issues trade and fiscal deficits of over 10 percent of GDP, a war whose costs seem limitless, and oil prices at multiyear highs, the resulting scenario is hardly conducive to low inflation and low interest rates.

Only one conclusion can be drawn from this state of affairs. Interest rates, after falling for over a generation, will now either

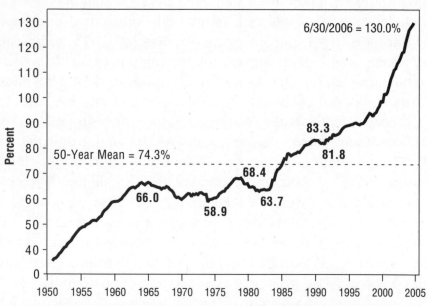

FIGURE 2.6   Household Debt as a Percentage of Disposable Personal Income

Source: Ned Davis Research. Used with permission. All rights reserved. Further distribution prohibited without prior written permission.

stay flat or rise. According to the *Economist,* the eventuality of rising interest rates can be further confirmed by recognizing that "the long-term real equilibrium interest rate should be equal to the marginal return on capital."[3] Due to several factors that are discussed later in this book (including globalization and the increasing relevance of emerging economies), the return on capital is rising, "so real interest rates should rise, not fall."[4] This will affect the real economy profoundly. And, as we have already seen from our previous analysis, any change in the real economy will also impact the financial economy.

Therefore, if we work under the reasonable assumption that, for the foreseeable future, interest rates are likely to remain flat or increase, then P/E ratios are likely to remain flat or decline.

Looking back to Figures 2.1 and 2.2, we can clearly see the implications of this P/E contraction as it relates to total market return. In other words, should overall equity returns remain positive in coming years, these returns will no longer be driven by P/E expansion, as was the case over the majority of the 1980 to 2000 period. Rather, returns will be driven by dividends and earnings.

So what does this have to do with free cash flow and Shareholder Yield? The next chapter provides the answer.

CHAPTER 3

Shareholder Yield in Depth

So far, we have endeavored to achieve the following goals: first, to provide a working definition of Shareholder Yield and, second, to explain why P/E is no longer the keystone metric that some investors continue to believe it is. But for any attentive reader, an important question remains: Even if the P/E ratio has ceased to be a positive explanatory variable in equity returns, why should Shareholder Yield necessarily emerge as a new driving force in the stock market?

In this chapter, we address this question by showing how recent market analyses, investment theories, and research support our conviction in a Shareholder Yield-dominated mechanism of future equity returns. By taking a closer look at how cash dividends, share buybacks, and debt paydowns function within today's marketplace, we can gain a deeper understanding of how to profit from the changing investment landscape.

Before we begin our investigation of cash dividends, the first component of Shareholder Yield, it is worth revisiting Figures 2.1 and 2.2, our three-variable depictions of the drivers of total equity market returns.

As outlined earlier, the data in Figures 2.1 and 2.2 provide the historical rationale behind the idea of Shareholder Yield.

Throughout the past eight decades, Dividends and EPS Growth have been consistently positive contributors to overall equity market return. In fact, during the years when P/E Change was falling or negative, Dividends and EPS Growth provided the S&P 500's only source of return expansion. The basic reason for this is obvious—since there are only three drivers of total return, two drivers (Dividends and EPS growth) should naturally come to prominence when and if the positive influence of the third driver (P/E Change) deteriorates.

Let's now take a moment to discuss the linkage between Shareholder Yield and the three drivers of total equity returns, as shown in Figures 2.1 and 2.2. Although they are not identified as specific drivers in their own right, the three components of Shareholder Yield each manifest themselves within this graph. Cash dividends are represented by the Dividends bar. Share repurchase, because it results in higher EPS, and debt repayment, because it decreases interest expense and therefore increases earnings, are incorporated within the EPS Growth bar.

At this point, the attentive reader will probably have the following consideration in mind. We've just spent a large part of Chapter 1 showing why earnings are an ineffectual way to gauge a company's performance and are therefore in opposition to the metrics derived by free cash flow and Shareholder Yield. How, then, can we say that share repurchase and debt paydowns (i.e., Shareholder Yield) are represented in our graph via EPS Growth (i.e., earnings)?

This is a valid query, and one for which the explanation is admittedly less than satisfactory. The reason we must express free cash flow- and finance-based concepts (share buybacks and debt paydowns) as part of an earnings- and accounting-based concept (EPS) is because earnings and their derivatives still dominate the qualitative and quantitative parlance of Wall Street. Despite the clear advantages of free cash flow, the metrics and data at our and the rest of the industry's disposal is still phrased in terms of earnings. In other words, most of the investment community still speaks the accountant's language. Figures 2.1 and 2.2, by necessity, are a reflection of this unfortunate reality.

Therefore, until our industry makes a full-scale shift to free cash flow standards, we must try our best to fit the three components of Shareholder Yield (based in finance) fit into our three-driver model of equity returns (based in accounting). Again, for our purposes, this will break down as follows: cash dividends are part of the dividends bar, and share buybacks and debt paydowns are part of the earnings bar. From this point forward, whenever we speak of the ascendancy of dividends and earnings as the drivers of total equity returns, you can accept this as a proxy for the ascendancy of free cash flow and Shareholder Yield. Hopefully, this proxy is only temporary. As the investment community continues to realize the importance of free cash flow, it is our hope that the set of available data and accepted industry lexicon will change accordingly.

To pick up where we left off a few paragraphs ago, we have entered a phase in the history of the equity markets during which P/E ratios are once again on the decline for the reasons outlined in the prior chapter. We need only look to the history of the equity markets to determine what will happen next.

We believe the future will be characterized by the emergence of free cash flow as the dominant metric in security selection, and this will be reflected by the increasing explanatory power of dividends and earnings (reinvested cash flows) as drivers of total equity returns. Today, an increasing number of investment professionals share our view that, "with portions of the economy showing signs of slowing, and a host of geopolitical and other concerns, how companies spend their cash—or don't—is becoming even more important."[1] Shareholder Yield, because it is based on notions of optimal free cash flow deployment, will therefore become a significant driving force in equity market returns.

It would be silly, however, to expect you to just take our or anyone else's word for it. To provide some tangible support for our assertion, let's look at what's been happening to cash dividends, the first component of Shareholder Yield. By establishing an anticipated trajectory for the size and prevalence of cash dividends, we can find an abundance of real-life evidence for this first facet of our investment philosophy.

Cash Dividends

The cash dividend is perhaps the most direct and immediate manner in which a company can return cash to shareholders. In addition to providing a tangible monetary return on an investment, dividends are important to shareholders because they "force management to be more thoughtful with corporate spending and to please longer-term shareholders; they are proof positive that cash is truly flowing through the organization."[2]

Throughout the history of the equity markets, the frequency and proportion of dividend payouts have shown a great deal of variation. However, within the past several years, there are signs that we have entered a period that has been and will remain quite friendly to the long-term viability of dividends as a free cash flow deployment strategy.

First, a little recent history. Prior to 2003, corporate dividends in the United States were subject to a 35 percent corporate income tax and an individual income tax of up to 38.6 percent. Among developed countries, only Japan levied a heavier tax on dividend income. As a result of these formerly stringent taxation policies, the number of U.S. companies paying dividends to their shareholders had steadily declined since the 1970s. For example, the percentage of large companies paying dividends in a given year fell from 68.5 percent in 1978 to 21.3 percent in 1998.[3]

However, as most investors are aware, the Jobs and Growth Tax Relief Reconciliation Act of 2003 included provisions to substantially reduce the individual tax on dividend income. Since the passage of this Act, dividend income to the individual investor has been taxed at 15 percent: a level that will remain in place until or beyond the Act's 2010 expiration date.

According to the American Shareholders Association, the effects of this dividend tax cut were already evident within the first 12 months of the lowered tax rates. From May 2003 to May 2004, there were 298 announcements of initial or increased dividend payments by firms in the S&P 500, compared with just 192 in the preceding year. In addition, net individual dividend income from S&P 500 firms increased 50 percent, from $32.7 billion in 2002 to $49.1 billion in 2003.[4]

Today, the 15 percent dividend tax rate has had several years to take hold, and the evidence for ongoing dividend growth continues to be very encouraging. After falling for two decades, the proportion of U.S. companies paying a dividend and the size of the dividends themselves have started to rise. Currently, around 386, or 77 percent, of the S&P 500 companies pay dividends, and this percentage could rise to around 85 percent over the next three years.[5] In 2005, companies in the S&P 500 paid out a record $202 billion in dividends and, according to Standard & Poor's, this number will increase to over $220 billion in 2006: a 9 percent increase over the prior year. Almost 300 of these dividend-paying companies increased the level of their dividend payout in 2005, while only 9 decreased it. Within the market as a whole, 1,949 dividend increases were announced in 2005, up 12 percent from 2004.

We believe this recent trend of impressive dividend growth, in combination with falling P/Es and rising interest rates, supports our confidence in the return-driving powers of Shareholder Yield. Anyone who follows the markets, however, knows that there is a big difference between a trend that is just gaining momentum and a trend that has already reached its peak. And, at this point, it is fair to ask whether the past several years of dividend growth represent a phenomenon that has meaningful staying power, or one whose effects have mostly come and gone. We believe that dividend growth belongs in the first category, and there is a great deal of empirical evidence that supports this claim.

A comparison between today's dividend payout ratios with historical averages provides a compelling picture of how dividends are poised for further expansion. Today, the average dividend payer in the S&P 500 is paying out about a third of its profits in dividends.[6] Contrast this to the historical dividend payout average of 56.6 percent since 1926 (see Figure 3.1) and it is easy to see that dividends still have plenty of room to grow.

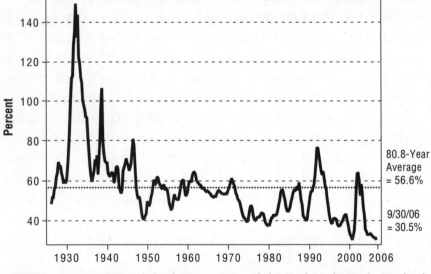

FIGURE 3.1   S&P 500 Dividend Payout Ratio (%): Trailing 4Q Cash Dividends/ Trailing 4Q Reported Earnings

Source: Ned Davis Research. Used with permission. All rights reserved. Further distribution prohibited without prior written permission.

In addition, the markets are and will continue to be primed for dividend-oriented cash deployment decisions. In other words, the current investment landscape is filled with companies with massive amounts of cash on hand. At the onset of 2005, cash represented more than 7 percent of the market value of the nonfinancial companies in the S&P 500, just short of a historical high. Additionally, today's "average corporate cash balance sits at a hefty $1 billion, up from $589 million four years ago."[7] Many of these cash-rich companies have learned the lessons of the 1990s in which ill-considered acquisitions led to negative consequences for both profits and share prices. Now, as these companies decide how to best deploy the growing amount of free cash flow on their books, they are looking for a strategy that will meaningfully benefit the shareholder and send positive signals to the market as a whole. Cash dividends have emerged as precisely such a strategy.

At this point, it serves our purposes to digress slightly into the realm of corporate finance and economic theory. We have already made a case for the dividend, not only as part of our Shareholder Yield-oriented investment strategy, but also as a significant contributor to the dynamics of today's marketplace. Now, however, we'd like to approach this topic from a slightly different angle in order to show yet another encouraging facet of this dividend story.

Investors and analysts have always argued about the value of the dividend. Often, the point of contention has revolved around whether or not the dividend, in and of itself, can serve as a meaningful signal for faster future earnings growth. There are many market observers who believe that the retention of cash for substantial internal reinvestment is the best way to generate earnings expansion. Therefore, in their view, low dividend payout ratios would signal higher earnings expectations. In other words, they would assert that dividends do not go hand in hand with earnings growth.

The opposite view is taken by Robert D. Arnott and Clifford S. Asness in "Surprise! Higher Dividends = Higher Earnings Growth," an article that appeared in the January/February 2003 issue of *Financial Analysts Journal*. To show that "expected future earnings growth is fastest when current [dividend] payout ratios are high and slowest when [dividend] payout ratios are low,"[8] Arnott and Asness looked at historical market data for dividend payout ratios and subsequent 10-year earnings growth. The dramatic correlation between the two can be seen in Figure 3.2.

According to the authors, the data in this chart provides empirical proof that dividend payouts and future earnings growth do *not* have an inverse relationship, as previously assumed by many market theorists. Rather, it shows that dividends have served as a historically robust indicator of overall market return. Arnott and Asness further extrapolate this find-

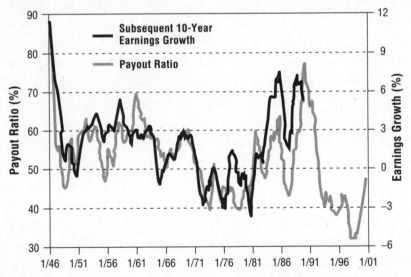

FIGURE 3.2   Payout Ratio and Subsequent 10-Year Earnings Growth, 1946–2001
Source: Robert D. Arnott and Clifford S. Asness, "Surprise! Higher Dividends = Higher Earnings Growth," *Financial Analysts Journal,* January/February 2003.

ing by showing that high P/Es can also signal earnings growth, but to a lesser degree than the link between dividend payouts and earnings growth. To quote the authors: "The power of market valuation levels [i.e. P/E] to forecast future return is weaker than the power of the [dividend] payout ratio—particularly in the modern period. For the post-WWII period, the difference is startling."[9] Put another way: "[Our] results . . . suggest that for forecasting future real earnings growth, look at managers' dividend policies rather than what the market will pay for each dollar of earnings. More often than not, it is the payout ratio, not the valuation level, that gets it right."[10] For those who subscribe to our belief in the ascendancy of Shareholder Yield, these findings could not be more encouraging.

And we're not the only ones who think so. According to *Barron's,* dividend-paying stocks in the S&P 500 have outperformed those that do not pay dividends since 1972.[11] Historical opinion is also on our side, as evidenced by investment gurus Benjamin Graham and David Dodd when they said in their previously mentioned 1934 guide to investing: "A successful company is one which will pay dividends regularly and presumably increase the rate as time goes on."[12] The data provided in Figure 3.3 point to a similar conclusion. It shows that, since the turn of the new millennium, stocks with the highest dividend yields have consistently outperformed nondividend-paying stocks as well as the S&P 500 as a whole.

Hopefully, it is now clear that, as P/Es cease to be a positive explanatory variable in equity market returns, other benchmarks such as dividend yield (and, by extension, share buybacks and debt paydowns) will emerge as increasingly meaningful investment drivers. To further explore the details of this investment thesis, let's move on to the second component of Shareholder Yield—share repurchases.

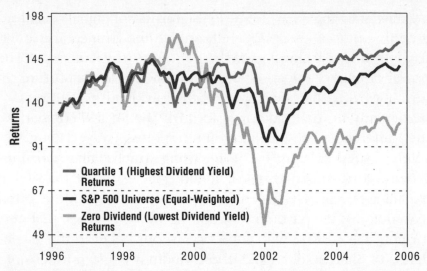

FIGURE 3.3   Performance of Stocks in S&P 500 with Highest Dividend Yields versus Lowest Dividend Yields versus Total S&P 500 Universe. Performance is equal-weighted (cross-sectional geometric). Rebalanced monthly.

Source: Ned Davis Research. Used with permission. All rights reserved. Further distribution prohibited without prior written permission.

Share Repurchases

Aside from cash dividends, share repurchases are the most immediately visible way in which a company can distribute cash to its shareholders. As in the case of dividends, share buybacks have also shown a dramatic recent upsurge in both frequency and magnitude. In fact, "a record profit cycle, cash-rich balance sheets, and investor demand has helped push the net buyback yield of the S&P 500 into record territory."[13]

It is no exaggeration to say that today's buyback activity is unprecedented in the history of the capital markets. Consider these statistics:

■ In 2005, companies in the S&P 500 spent a record $349 billion on buybacks. This is up 77 percent from $197 billion in 2004,[14] a number that, at the time, was also a record. At the present run rate, according to Standard & Poor's, buybacks will reach a record $410 billion in 2006, an increase of 17 percent over the prior year.

■ In the S&P 500, 68 percent of companies repurchased shares in 2005, the highest percentage since 1985.[15]

■ Within the market as a whole, 1,012 U.S.-based companies spent a record $456 billion on buybacks in 2005. The previous record was set in 2004, during which 728 companies spent $312 on buybacks.[16]

■ Today, net stock repurchases are nearly triple 1999 to 2000 levels.[17]

Figures 3.4 and 3.5 show how this striking increase in share buybacks has gained momentum over the past two years.

Figure 3.6 on page 51 uses a longer time period to show this buyback growth as a percentage of gross cash flow.

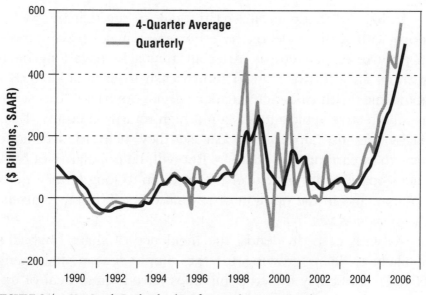

FIGURE 3.4   Net Stock Buybacks (Nonfinancial Corporations)
Source: JPMorgan.

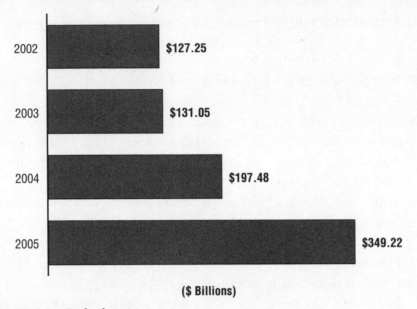

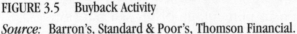

FIGURE 3.5   Buyback Activity
Source: Barron's, Standard & Poor's, Thomson Financial.

In light of this data, it isn't difficult to see that buybacks, along with cash dividends, have become a major driving force in positive equity returns. After all, buybacks have long been seen as an effective way to return cash to shareholders. For companies with cash-rich balance sheets, buybacks "can serve as an effective vehicle to sustain a high return on equity. Buybacks are also appealing because they help to accelerate growth of earnings per share."[18] But will the popularity of buybacks continue to grow over the medium to long term? In our opinion, and in the opinion of several other industry analysts, the answer is yes.

As with cash dividends, the incidence of share buybacks is likely to keep growing for the simple reason that many of today's publicly traded companies have a great deal of excess cash on hand. To quote an analyst report from earlier this year: "With cash balances at nonfinancial companies (with or

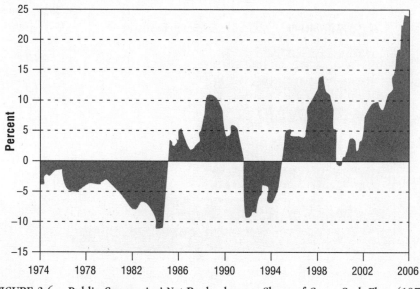

FIGURE 3.6   Public Companies' Net Buybacks as a Share of Gross Cash Flow (1974 through Early August 2006).

Source: Corporate Reports, Empirical Research Partners Analysis.

without the Energy sector) up to 8.5 percent of market capitalization, and *still growing* with profits, these massive share repurchases could stay at present levels for years unless other demands on cash emerge, such as a faster pace of capital investment."[19]

It is no coincidence that this evidence for share buybacks sounds remarkably familiar to our discussion of cash dividends. Both of these cash deployment strategies represent an effective way to distribute cash to shareholders and, because of this, the market has seen a large and growing increase in both dividends and buybacks. In fact, by viewing these strategies as two peas in the same corporate finance pod, the evidence for their continued popularity grows even stronger.

Consider, for instance, the data represented in Figure 3.7.[20]

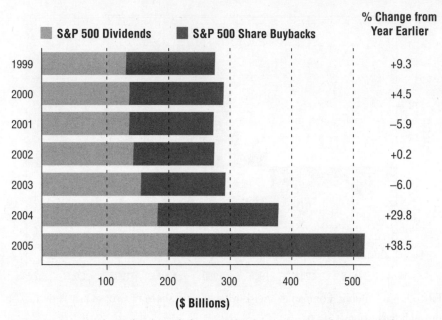

FIGURE 3.7   Total Dividends and Share Buybacks in S&P 500 (1999–2005)
Source: Standard & Poor's, *New York Times.*

Figure 3.7 shows the combined historical levels of dividends and share buybacks. As discussed earlier, the past two years have seen substantial recent increases in both of these phenomena that, if taken in aggregate, point to an even more definitive market trend. According to the *New York Times:* "If one views buybacks as a form of dividend, then the combined payouts for both 2004 and 2005 produced yields on year-end values of 4.6 percent—figures that in the old days would have been seen as an indication that stocks were a good buy."[21] According to another equity strategist, this "real yield" is at its highest level since the early 1990s.[22] Indeed, " 'shareholder enhancements' (a fancy name for dividends plus share buybacks), are at a five-year high and have surpassed capital expenditure as a preferred use of cash. While the average annual dividend payment has doubled to $502 million since 2002, the average share repurchase has virtually tripled to $612 million."[23] In fact, "buybacks have become so pervasive that net buyback yield (i.e., net buybacks less share issuance) of the S&P 500 is now equal to the index's dividend yield. This is the first instance of such a convergence in . . . 20 years."[24]

Share buybacks, therefore, serve not only as a signal of a management team's confidence in the investment worthiness of its own stock, but also as a cash deployment strategy that matches the yield-creating power of cash dividends. For this reason, the concept of Shareholder Yield serves to capture the growing importance of buybacks as a method of returning cash to shareholders.

We ended our discussion of cash dividends by referencing the world of academia, and we hope it will be helpful to do the same as we come to the conclusion of our section on stock buybacks. David L. Ikenberry, a finance professor at the University of Illinois at Urbana-Champaign, has found that the correlation between buyback activity and expected return is similar to the link between dividend payouts and earnings growth shown by Arnott and Asness. That is, the stock prices of companies that announce buybacks tend to outperform those that do not, in the same way that companies with high dividend payout ratios tend to reap faster earnings growth than those with low payout ratios. In an as-yet unpublished study,[25] Ikenberry examined the stock price performance of 7,725 companies who announced share buybacks between 1980 and 2000. Ikenberry and his team discovered that, after a four-year holding period, investors who owned these stocks realized a return that was 15.6 percent higher than a similar portfolio of stocks that might or might not have engaged in buyback activity. Ikenberry's results point, yet again, to a marketplace in which share buybacks, in addition to the other two components of Shareholder Yield, play an increasingly central role in driving equity market returns.

Debt Repayment

The final component of Shareholder Yield—debt repayment—is another way in which a company can return cash or "pay a dividend" to the shareholder. However, the reasoning behind our inclusion of debt repayment in Shareholder Yield is slightly less straightforward than our earlier explanations of cash dividends and share repurchases. As a result, we change our tactics slightly in this section and, instead of providing a list of data and statistics, we provide two case studies that we hope more effectively validate the theory behind the dividend-yielding powers of debt paydowns.

To preface these case studies, let's first revisit the theories put forth by Modigliani and Miller. As you may recall from our discussion in Chapter 2, Modigliani and Miller's Nobel Prize-winning paper in finance proved that the value of a corporation is independent of its capital structure, provided that the effect of taxes on the deductibility of interest is ignored.[26] To put this in mathematical terms, assume that we have two streams of cash flow, A and B. It follows that the present value of A + B is equal to the present value of A plus the present value of B. Now assume that A is debt and B is equity. In this case, if a dollar of free cash flow is paid to reduce the debt level (A), since Modigliani and Miller assert that the NPV(A + B) = NPV(A⁻ + B), this reduction in debt becomes additive to the present value of B (equity) so long as the total cash flows of the firm remain the same.

Now that we have reacquainted ourselves with Modigliani and Miller, let's look at a company that has effectively put this theory into practice. KFI Industries is a manufacturer of wheels, brakes, and other components serving the commercial airline, business jet, and defense markets. In August of 2005, KFI went public through an IPO. Since that time, KFI has managed to make positive strides within its industry. The company has a large market share on high cycle aircraft and is often the sole-source provider, thereby allowing for high (30 percent or higher) operating margins. According to the research firm Stifel Nicolas, KFI has content on 26,000 aircraft and is a sole-source provider of wheels and brakes for 75 percent of its customer base.

However, the company also carries a high debt to capital ratio (over 50 percent). KFI's management has expressed unease with this significant amount of leverage and has indicated that much of the company's free cash flow will be used to pay down debt. With its free cash flow growing at high single-digit rates, a wealth transfer will occur between the debt holder and the equity holder as KFI uses its funds to liquidate debt. Under Modigliani and Miller's argument, the value of the business is unchanged given the constant level of cash flows, and the equity holder benefits from the debt paydown on a dollar for dollar basis.

Our next example is a company that employs two of the three cash flow deployment options within Shareholder Yield— share repurchase and debt paydown—to create shareholder value. The company is Davita, a provider of dialysis services in the United States for patients suffering from chronic kidney failure, also known as end stage renal disease. Davita operates kidney centers and provides related medical services in dialysis centers and contracted hospitals across the country.

Many investors avoided purchasing Davita stock because of the company's business characteristics. Specifically, Davita generates low unit growth, more or less in line with the incidence of the disease, combined with a great deal of industry regulation. In addition, the prices the company is able to charge its customers are subject to statutory regulation and insurance company reimbursement policies, which results in price increases that are small and infrequent in nature. Despite these potential hindrances to profitability, Davita has shown itself to be a very good operator; the company's management team has been able to grow operating cash flow at a faster rate than revenues for several years.

Most encouragingly, between 2001 and 2005, management used most of its free cash flow to buy back stock, reducing the shares outstanding from almost 150 million in 2001 to just over 103 million in 2006. On a per share basis, it is easy to see how Davita's stock price has been positively impacted by rising cash flow per share. As investors, we were happy to see that this increase in share price was the direct result of the application of a Shareholder Yield-oriented strategy.

But the story continues. In 2005, Davita purchased a similar business, GAMBRO. The acquisition was largely debt financed. Because Davita has already shown itself to be a subscriber to the Shareholder Yield philosophy, we anticipate that a large amount of the company's free cash flow will now be directed toward debt paydown. As in the case of KFI, this decision will result in a shift of value from the debt holder to the equity owner. Since cash flows determine firm value, this shift in the company's capital structure will change the composition of the company's total value, but not the total value itself.

The data in Figure 3.8 provides evidence that Davita's focus on Shareholder Yield has already paid off. Over the past four years, the company's shareholders have benefited from owning shares in a business that does not appear attractive on the surface, but is greatly strengthened by its underlying commitment to effective free cash flow generation and deployment.

In our discussion of debt paydowns, it is important to note that, while the examples of KFI and Davita are certainly indicative of a trend in free cash flow deployment, it is a trend that is not yet as evident in the marketplace as the trends of cash dividends and share repurchase. This is because the opportunity for debt repayment isn't currently as big as the opportunities for dividend payments and share buybacks. In today's market,

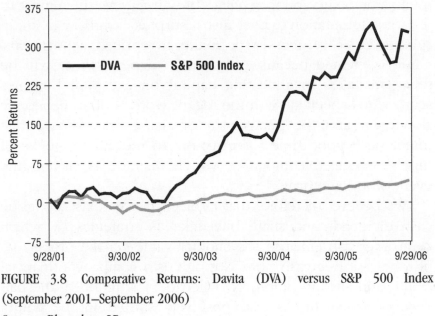

FIGURE 3.8 Comparative Returns: Davita (DVA) versus S&P 500 Index (September 2001–September 2006)

Source: Bloomberg LP.

the debt held by public U.S. companies is relatively low compared to historical averages. According to Standard and Poor's, "high profits and low interest rates have allowed nonfinancial corporations to reduce leverage ratios significantly."[27] This, in combination with high cash balances, has resulted in smaller amounts of debt outstanding and, therefore, fewer instances of repayment.

Today's low levels of public corporate debt, however, do not negate the inclusion of debt repayment within the dividend-producing tactics that comprise Shareholder Yield. The benefits of debt repayment remain clear, regardless of the frequency with which this strategy is employed. Unless a company exists within a highly regulated industry (such as the utility industry), the simple fact remains that it is dangerous and potentially harmful to shareholder interests to have a balance sheet that carries a lot of debt. This is why debt repayment can signal that the management team is on the right track: "the obligation to repay debt will remove the almost irresistible temptation to over-invest surplus cash flow in undeserving basic businesses or make overpriced acquisitions. Value is created because the market expects there will be fewer mistakes in allocating capital once capital becomes scarcer."[28] Especially with the recent worries of an economic slowdown and the persistence of rising interest rates, "it might be a good time for investors to reevaluate stocks of highly leveraged companies, which may be at risk in the event of a downturn."[29]

We believe, therefore, that debt paydowns exist alongside cash dividends and share buybacks as strategies by which companies can enhance shareholder value via the proper deployment of free cash flow. Not only is a company's financial health and stability improved when debt is reduced, the balance of ownership is also positively shifted in the equity holder's direction.

In summary, this chapter has addressed the reasoning behind and the evidence for the increasing relevance of a Shareholder Yield-based approach to equity investing. In the next chapter, we return to the topic of cash dividends in order to provide some additional explanations for the growing popularity of this specific cash deployment strategy.

Focus on Dividends

In Chapter 3, we examined how several directly observable market trends could be cited in support of the growing importance of dividends and the manner in which they are positioned to play an especially prominent role in the ascendance of Shareholder Yield. Now, in Chapter 4, we'd like to expand that argument to include some dividend-oriented predictions for corporate behavior, specifically in the realm of private equity investment and executive compensation strategies.

First, let's review our three-variable equation for total market return. The change in total return for any equity index can be defined as follows: dividends plus EPS growth plus P/E change. As discussed earlier, dividends have always been an important contributor to overall equity returns. However, from 1980 through 2000, their contribution was relatively minor. During this 20-year period, P/E expansion and earnings growth accounted for over 80 percent of the return in the stock market, as indicated in Table 4.1.

Today, this equation is changing, largely due to interest rates that are no longer falling. As discussed in prior chapters, P/E ratios rise when interest rates fall and vice versa. Since June of 2003, interest rates have been more likely to rise than

TABLE 4.1   Total Return for Equities 1980–2000

P/E Change	7.6%
EPS Growth	6.4
Dividends	3.6
Total annualized return	17.6%

fall and, hence, P/E ratios are more likely to fall than rise. As a result, earnings growth and dividend yield have become the dominant drivers of future equity returns. Specifically, dividends—in the form of cash, stock buybacks, or debt paydowns—will soon comprise nearly half of the total return expected from equities, up from 20 percent for the period 1980 to 2000.

So, cash dividends, as we have learned in prior chapters, are poised to play an increasingly meaningful role in total equity returns. Figure 4.1 provides further evidence that this is the case.

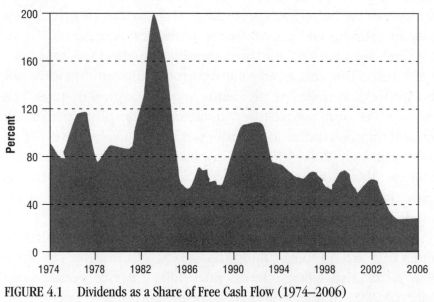

FIGURE 4.1   Dividends as a Share of Free Cash Flow (1974–2006)
Source: Corporate Reports, Empirical Research Partners Analysis.

Figure 4.1 shows the relationship between cash dividends and free cash flow levels for U.S. corporations over the past 30 years. The dividend-to-free-cash-flow ratio is currently at a 30 year low. In other words, the capability to increase dividends has never been better than it is today. In our view, this justifies an investment perspective that places a growing importance on the role of dividends in a company's free cash flow deployment strategy.

To fully consider this dividend-oriented investment perspective, we must ask whether firms will actually pay higher dividends just because they have the capability to do so. In our view, the answer is yes. For evidence, we can cite the data in the previous chapter. To provide further support for the onset of higher and more frequent dividend payments, we'd like to add two extra considerations into the mix.

First, dividend payouts have become, in part, a de facto protection mechanism against the takeover aspirations of private equity investors. In many cases, dividends are the best possible use of free cash flow. As pointed out previously, if a dollar of free cash flow cannot be put to work by a company at the same or higher rate of return currently being earned on the capital employed in the business, then that incremental dollar should be returned to the shareholder through dividends. Technically, this can take the form of cash, stock buybacks, or debt paydowns. If a company's current management team fails to make efficient use of its assets in this manner, there are other management teams who will be more than happy to do it for them. These "other" management teams are often private equity investors, who have recently amassed billions of dollars specifically earmarked for the takeover of companies that do not use their cash, working capital, and other assets efficiently. These private equity investors will use the target company's cash—cash that might have been used for dividends—to reduce the cost of acquisition. As a result, the company's decision to retain cash instead of returning it to shareholders becomes part of the impetus behind the private equity takeover. With less cash on the books, however, and more free cash put to use through dividend mechanisms, the company might not have been acquired. Today, there is ample evidence that this is taking place as more and more cash-rich companies "buy back shares—if only to keep private-equity groups at bay. Such buybacks surged to $117 billion in the second quarter [of 2006], according to the Bank for International Settlements, compared with a quarterly average of $87 billion [in 2005]."[1] For these reasons, we believe that today's robust private equity market provides a clear incentive for the intelligent use of a company's free cash flow by its management team.

Today's changing corporate compensation system is another compelling reason for management teams to increase dividends, particularly of the "cash" variety. Options were a popular compensation strategy for many years, mostly from 1980 through 2000 when falling interest rates created huge windfalls for corporate executives and options were not required to be expensed under the rules of GAAP. Now, however, interest rates are more likely to rise than fall, and changes in accounting principles have dictated that options must be expensed. As a result, the usage of options is currently on the decline. Both Citicorp and Exxon, for example, have eliminated their option plans.

The fact that options have fallen out of favor is part of the reasoning behind the emergence of restricted stocks units (RSUs) as a significant component of compensation packages. Generally speaking, RSUs are exactly like the shares of a company available for public purchase, but they are awarded to a firm's employees and often have vesting restrictions and occasionally sales restrictions. However, if the firm pays a dividend, most RSU plans allow all shareholders, including members of the company's management team, to receive that cash in the same way that general shareholders would regardless of the percentage vested. This cash is taxed at a rate of 15 percent, which is lower than the rate applicable to bonuses.

Therefore, RSUs represent a compensation-related incentive for companies to pay dividends that did not exist previously. For example, suppose there was a company with management's options struck at $45, a company market price of $40, and excess cash of $5 per share on the balance sheet. Paying a special dividend of $5 could leave the option holder $10, rather than $5, away from realizing his or her option value. Therefore, a potential bias to retain cash, if it indeed existed at all, has disappeared with the arrival of RSUs. With RSUs, all shareholders receive the benefits of dividends, including management. RSUs, therefore, provide yet another compelling rationale behind the dividend-related deployment of free cash flow.

Conclusion

Now that we have come to the end of Part One, we'd like to briefly summarize the key points of the past several chapters. First, we addressed the disparities between accounting and finance in order to show how accounting-based concepts of earnings and P/Es are fundamentally flawed and should therefore not be considered reliable investment metrics. Second, we discussed the changing order of the drivers of total equity return and put forth a scenario under which interest rates are more likely to be flat or rising rather than falling, causing P/E ratios to be flat or declining. In light of both of these considerations—the inaccuracies of the P/E ratio as a metric and its decreasing contributions to equity returns—we introduced the concept of Shareholder Yield, which reflects the application of free cash flow as a preferred investment metric. Then, we explained how the three components of Shareholder Yield—cash dividends, share buybacks, and debt paydowns—are gaining momentum in today's marketplace. All of this has been done with one objective in mind: to help the informed investor approach the equity markets with a clear and effective set of free cash flow-based investment criteria.

In Part Two of the book, we expand this discussion to address several key trends and themes within the global investment landscape. As you read Part Two, keep the concept of Shareholder Yield in mind. In doing so, you should be able to see how a focus on free cash flow and an understanding of the likelihood of flat or rising interest rates should clarify the opportunities and challenges of a changing international marketplace.

PART TWO

The New
Investment Landscape

CHAPTER 5

Globalization

Even though a primary goal of this book is to advocate the specific idea of Shareholder Yield, we believe it is also important to acquire a larger understanding of the global financial environment as a whole. After all, nothing can exist in a vacuum, and Shareholder Yield is no exception. For this reason, Part Two is dedicated to addressing several key investment challenges and opportunities within the changing international marketplace.

To start this discussion, the idea of globalization provides an obvious jumping-off point. Much has already been made of this concept—both in the investment world and otherwise—and we are among the many who recognize its extreme importance.* For this reason, Chapter 5 provides an investment-specific analysis of how globalization has and will affect the capital markets. In this chapter, we highlight globalization-related trends and concepts of particular interest and we link these ideas to specific portfolio management solutions. Furthermore, we reinforce the importance of an international perspective and

---

* An excellent primer on the subject is Thomas Friedman's *The World Is Flat: A Brief History of the Twenty-First Century* (New York: Farrar, Straus and Giroux, 2005).

suggest how globalization may impact the investment landscape going forward.

The Law of Comparative Advantage

As investors, everything we once knew about the world—and our place in it—is changing. Prior to the fall of the Berlin Wall in 1989, the investor's world largely consisted of Europe, Japan, and the United States. From a strictly economic perspective, China, India, Russia, and the rest of the world's population mattered little. With the collapse of the Berlin Wall in 1989, however, the marketplace's physical and psychological boundaries began to disintegrate. Since that time, globalization has accelerated at an unprecedented pace, creating an increasingly borderless marketplace for goods, services, information, labor, and capital. Today, influential new players like China, India, Russia, and Brazil—the same countries that were once financial nonentities—are appearing on the world's economic stage, resulting in a transition within the global interrelationships of capital, labor, and technology.

This transition is particularly evident in the rapid growth of tradable goods and services. Global trade has nearly doubled its share of world GDP since 1986. In 2005, world exports as a percentage of world GDP—a ratio that serves as a proxy for world trade—grew to 28.53 percent from 16.92 percent in 1986, an increase of nearly 70 percent.[1] Furthermore, capitalism has emerged in one form or another throughout the world, which means that a single economic ideology is now driving global trade and resource allocations: a development that is reinforced by the dissemination of an international "rule of law" by institutions such as the World Trade Organization (WTO).

In short, the world is becoming one huge marketplace in which the forces of capitalism are working to efficiently utilize capital and labor. How, then, will this new international paradigm work itself out? The answer lies in the Law of Comparative Advantage, an understanding of which is crucial to an informed discussion of globalization.

The Law of Comparative Advantage was developed by English economist David Ricardo (1772–1823) in 1820. This law states that "if each nation specializes in the production of goods in which it has a comparative cost advantage and then trades with other nations for the goods in which they specialize, there will be an overall gain in trade, and overall income levels should rise in each trading country."[2]

To introduce the manner in which this law functions, let's take a look at three very illustrative images. The first of these images (Figure 5.1) shows how the world would look if a country's size was directly proportional to its population

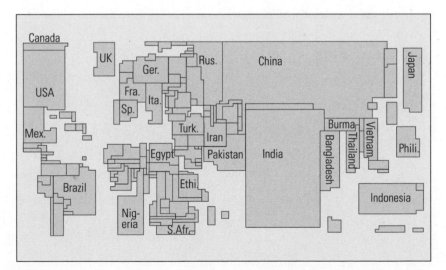

FIGURE 5.1   Demographic and Political Changes: Current Population Comparisons

density. It is easy to see that, by redrawing the world's borders in this manner, we arrive at a radically different picture of global geography.

Figure 5.2 takes Figure 5.1 a step further by showing what this picture would look like in approximately a generation, when the population density in countries like China and India are anticipated to become even more extreme.

Finally, Figure 5.3 redraws the world's borders once again by showing what would happen if each nation's size was dependant on the magnitude of its gross domestic product (GDP).

If we compare Figures 5.1 and 5.2 to Figure 5.3, we can see some remarkable disparities between population density and GDP, particularly in countries such as India and China, where population and productivity are on opposite ends of the numerical scale. Table 5.1 on page 72 shows this in quantitative form by ranking countries according to the ratio of GDP per capita.

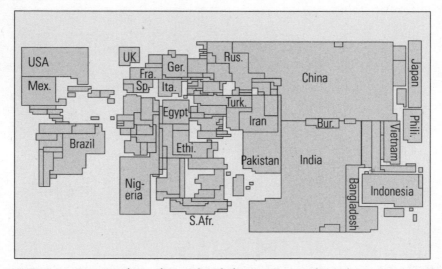

FIGURE 5.2   Demographic and Geopolitical Changes: Projected Population Comparisons

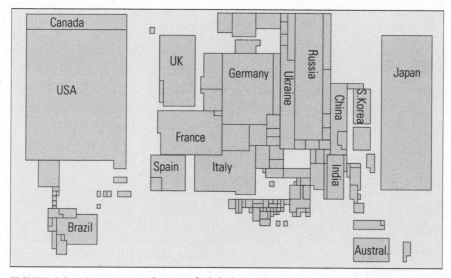

FIGURE 5.3   Current Distribution of Global Wealth by Gross Domestic Product

Now, let's figure out how, in this new boundary-free world of spreading capitalism, these disparities will equalize. To do so, there are two variables we need to consider: labor and capital.

First, we'll focus on labor. Take another look at those low GDP per capita numbers in places like China, India, and other developing countries: In most cases, these numbers reflect wages of less than $1 an hour. Conversely, hourly wages in the West are around $20 per hour. Therefore, assuming that our world will continue to be governed by the open policies of globalization, it is easy to see why industries whose operations require high labor inputs will naturally move to India, China, and the like. Anyone who reads the newspapers knows that this is already happening and will continue to happen at an extremely rapid pace. Additionally, industries that require technology, education, and capital (in other words, more than just labor) will tend to remain localized in the West, where

TABLE 5.1   2005 GDP and GDP per Capita

Country	GDP ($billion)	GDP per Capita ($)
United States	12,970	43,740
Japan	4,988	38,980
United Kingdom	2,264	37,600
France	2,178	34,810
Germany	2,852	34,580
Russia	639	4,460
Brazil	644	3,460
China	2,264	1,740
India	793	720

Source: World Development Indicators database, World Bank, OECD.

technology, education, and capital are available in relative abundance.

So far, much of this may sound like a repeat of things that you, as an informed investor, already know. Where it gets fun and interesting—in our opinion, at least—is when we relate the dynamics of our new global marketplace to that old and venerable economic law: the Law of Comparative Advantage. Put very simply, the relationship between globalization and the Law of Comparative Advantage can be explained as follows: "Consumers see globalization as the chance to buy inexpensive t-shirts, furniture, or appliances made in faraway factories. For companies [or countries], the phenomenon means the ability to divide both the production and the distribution of their products into discrete tasks."[3] More specifically, as noted earlier, the Law of Comparative Advantage states that each nation should specialize in making whatever goods and services it makes well. That is, each nation should focus its efforts on the tasks for which it has a relative production advantage. Then, each nation should trade those goods and services for other

TABLE 5.2   Products and Labor Costs

Product	Country A	Country B
1 unit of food	1 days' labor	3 days' labor
1 unit of clothing	2 days' labor	4 days' labor

goods and services it desires. If every nation follows this maxim, all countries are far better off than if they tried to meet their needs through internal production alone.

The following example will provide an illustration of the Law of Comparative Advantage at work. Imagine a world of two countries with only two products—food and clothing. Labor costs are known for each country. Let us also assume that food and clothing are equally valued in both counties such that there is a desire to have the same amount of each good within each country. Table 5.2 shows each country's comparative advantage in food and clothing production.

Based on the ratios in Table 5.2, we can assume that, if each country spent 100 days to internally produce all the necessary units of food and clothing for its own needs, the total number of units of food and clothing would be 94, as shown in Table 5.3.

TABLE 5.3   Internal Production Only

Product	Country A 100 Days	Country B 100 Days	Total
Food	$\dfrac{1/3 \times 100}{1} = 33$ units	$\dfrac{3/7 \times 100}{3} = 14$ units	47 units
Clothing	$\dfrac{2/3 \times 100}{2} = 33$ units	$\dfrac{4/7 \times 100}{4} = 14$ units	47 units
Total	66 units	28 units	94 units

In other words, because of its overall efficiency, Country A can produce 66 units whereas Country B can produce only 28 units, which brings us to a total of 94. However, according to the Law of Comparative Advantage, what really matters is not the *absolute* efficiency of Country A relative to Country B, but the *relative* efficiency of each country in the production of each good.

For instance, Country A has a much greater advantage in food production compared to Country B than it does in clothing production (1 to 3 versus 2 to 4, according to Table 5.2). This being the case, common sense tells us that Country A should therefore emphasize food production, so long as it can trade with Country B to gain the required units of clothing it seeks. This, in a nutshell, is the solution dictated by the Law of Comparative Advantage.

Table 5.4 shows us how the aggregate productivity of these countries would change if the Law was put into effect.

Under this new scenario, a larger total number of food and clothing units are produced (100 units versus 94 units). However, this outcome also illustrates why the process of globalization and producing to comparative advantage could create a significant backlash in places like Country B. As you can see from Table 5.4, the total number of food units produced in Country B under the Law of Comparative Advantage is zero,

TABLE 5.4   Producing to Comparative Advantage

Product	Country A 100 Days	Country B 100 Days	Total
Food	$\dfrac{50}{1 \text{ day}} = 50$ units	0	50 units
Clothing	$\dfrac{50}{2 \text{ days}} = 25$ units	$\dfrac{100}{4 \text{ days}} = 25$ units	50 units
Total	75 units	25 units	100 units

where it once was 14. This means that, as a result of globalization, the food workers in Country B are unemployed. To the extent they have skills in producing units of clothing rather than units of food, they can migrate to the clothing industry for employment. Still, not all workers will be able to achieve this outcome and will therefore remain unemployed, creating a new social dilemma for the leaders and populace of Country B. However, because of the overall benefits of globalization, Country B now has more wealth at its disposal and can therefore afford to provide assistance such as job training or pensions to the displaced food workers. In doing so, however, Country B will have to evaluate the programs and policies to be put in place to protect the displaced so as to avoid losing the overall gain received from participating in the globalization process.

To return to the outcome expressed in Table 5.4, it is evident that, if both countries produced to comparative advantage, 100 units of food and clothing would be created, which is six more than under the previous scenario. Since Country A is so much more efficient overall than Country B, Country A would end up with most of these six incremental units, but not all of them. Arguably, Country A would reserve several of its incremental units to trade with Country B. Country B would not entertain trading with A unless it received a benefit. Since A is roughly three times more productive than B, it is reasonable to assume the incremental six units produced in this example would be shared proportionally. For our purposes, let us assume that would be two-thirds to A and one-third to B. This outcome is illustrated in Table 5.5.

Through this example, we can see how Country A and Country B would both be better off under the Law of Comparative Advantage. In the real world, the application of this Law has been facilitated through globalization, and it has already produced dramatic results.

TABLE 5.5   Reconfiguring Total to Reflect A's Relative Production Advantage to B (75/25 = 3:1)

Product	Country A	Country B	Total
Food	35 units	15 units	50 units
Clothing	35 units	15 units	50 units
Total	70 units	30 units	100 units

Labor and the "Positive Supply-Side Shock"

To continue this discussion, let's return to the labor/wage arbitrage situation that was introduced earlier in this chapter in which labor-requiring industries in the West took advantage of the lower wages in developing countries. How is this labor/capital relationship playing out as globalization and the Law of Comparative Advantage continue to take effect? In the words of Harvard economist Richard Freeman, the international labor market has recently undergone a "positive supply-side shock" as a result of the entrance of the BRIC countries (Brazil, Russia, India, and China) into the new globalized economy. These new entrants have brought little capital with them, but a huge amount of available labor. Hence, we now have twice the amount of workers with the same amount of available capital. With the addition of the BRIC countries to the international labor force, the ratio of capital to labor has fallen by 50 percent, probably the largest change in history. It is this ratio that determines the relative returns to labor and capital, and also helps to explain the recent trends in wages and profits. Real wage growth and wages as a percentage of national income have been weak in the West's developed countries, but profits and returns on capital have been very high as a result of capital's relative scarcity. In fact, corporate profits in the G7 countries are at 25-year highs, showing a 50 percent increase over 1980, as shown in Figure 5.4.

Taken together, the changing international relationship between labor and capital has increased the growth potential for countries throughout the world, has helped hold down inflation, and has caused huge changes in the relative prices of capital, goods, and assets. We believe that these positive trends are direct evidence of the application of the Law of Comparative Advantage. Not only has the law caused a boom in corporate profits as seen in Figure 5.4, it is also at the heart of the steady increase in the world's GDP numbers provided by the International Monetary Fund (IMF). The rise of 5.3 percent in the world's GDP in 2005, the fastest growth rate in 20 years, is attributable to the law at work. Because of globalization and the Law of Comparative Advantage, "emerging economies have become more integrated into the global system of production,

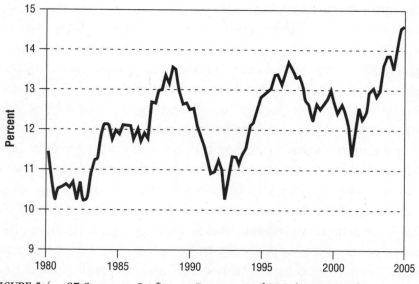

FIGURE 5.4   G7 Corporate Profits as a Percentage of GDP (1980–2005)
Source: UBS.

with trade and capital flows accelerating relative to GDP in the past 10 years."[4] In fact, "since 2000, world GDP per head has grown by an average of 3.2 percent a year, thanks to the acceleration of emerging economies." This 3.2 percent may seem to be insignificant, but it is actually the opposite. Continued per capita growth at this rate would result in a doubling of today's living standards in just 24 years. Barring the institution of tariffs and import quotas, this phenomenon would be wide-ranging and long lasting, and would benefit the living standards of us all.

Globalization via the Law of Comparative Advantage also provides further support for our expectation of flat or rising interest rates that, in turn, further validates our focus on free cash flow and Shareholder Yield. This argument unfolds as follows: Real interest rates should roughly track real GDP growth rates, which is a proxy for real return on capital. Therefore, "if greater global economic and financial integration leads to a more efficient use of labor and capital [i.e., the Law of Comparative Advantage], economic growth will be faster, which . . . means that real interest rates should rise."[5]

Having cited this example, it is necessary to linger briefly on this point in order to avoid potential confusion in upcoming pages. We've just stated that globalization should cause real interest rates to remain flat or rise, and this is indeed the case. But there are also aspects of the globalization process that may put downward pressure on interest rates, and we believe this phenomenon exists alongside the prior one. To explain how this works, it is necessary to understand the general concept of interest rates. Specifically, the nominal interest rate is equal to the real interest rate plus a measure that reflects inflation. (In this book, the term *interest rate* is used to refer to the nominal interest rate unless specifically indicated otherwise.) Globalization affects the nominal interest rate and the real interest rate in different ways. As mentioned in the prior paragraph, globalization has resulted in higher worldwide GDPs and, because *real* interest rates have been shown to track historical GDP growth, it follows that *real* interest rates should rise as well. However, at the same time, globalization has also lowered wage expenses via the labor arbitrage phenomenon inherent in the Law of Comparative Advantage. These low wages have resulted in low prices, which has kept inflation down. Therefore, if we add this decrease in inflation to the increase in *real* interest rates, we end up with *nominal* interest rates that will rise, fall, or stay the same by virtue of the magnitude of these two independent variables. For the purposes of the investment perspective presented in this book, we believe the positive contribution of real growth from climbing world GDPs will combine with the negative contribution of low inflation to result in nominal interest rate levels which, at this point in time, are likely to follow a flat-to-growing trajectory, but will be kept lower than they otherwise would be without the presence of labor arbitrage and its impact on inflation measures.

Now, let's return to our discussion of globalization. The integration of over three billion people from developing countries into the world's economy is indeed a powerful stimulant to the international investment landscape. Today's developing countries accounted for more than half of total world GDP in 2005.[6] These developing economies have not yet been able to fully flex their muscles; after all, they are still "developing." But, in the words of the *Economist:*

> As these newcomers become more integrated into the global economy and their incomes catch up with the rich countries, they will provide the biggest boost to the world economy since the industrial revolution. Indeed, it is likely to be the biggest stimulus in history, because the industrial revolution fully involved only one-third of the world's population. By contrast, this new revolution covers most of the globe, so the economic gains—as well as the pains—will be far bigger.[7]

In our view, China is the epicenter of this remarkable phenomenon. The next section in this chapter deals specifically with how China is positioned to radically alter the dynamics of the international economy.

China

It is difficult to overstate the growing importance of China's role within the global marketplace. America's relative economic superiority and power are slipping away just as China's prominence is ascending, as pointed out by Clyde Prestowitz in his book *Three Billion New Capitalists*. "China is like the new sun in the solar system, pulling the balance of world power back toward the East for the first time"[8] in almost six hundred years; and it's happening at a staggering pace. For the skeptics out there, consider this statistic: "When America and Britain were industrializing in the 19th century, they took 50 years to double their real incomes per head; today China is achieving the same feat in nine years."[9]

The following data will help to underscore the magnitude and rapidity of China's ascendancy. China's GDP was recently adjusted upward to $2.2 trillion for 2005, compared with $12 to $13 trillion in the United States, making it the world's fourth largest economy after the United States, Japan, and Germany. At the present respective growth rates for the United States and China, the GDP gap between these two countries could be closed in two generations. In terms of purchasing power parity, China could have a larger GDP than the United States in just 15 years and, in terms of nominal GDP, China could surpass the United States by the year 2040. Furthermore, China accounts for nearly 20 percent of the incremental growth in the world's economy, ranking second only to the United States.

In terms of global trade, China is gaining power by becoming everyone's biggest customer, as evidenced by their rise to the status of fourth largest economy in the world. Similarly, Chinese exports have grown more than eightfold since 1990 and its current share of global exports exceeds 7 percent compared to less than 4 percent in 2000. It has surpassed the United States as the biggest export market for South Korea, Taiwan, Japan, and Indonesia.

In addition, China has attracted over $600 billion in foreign direct investment ($79 billion in 2005 alone) over the past 16 years, and output from China's private sector now approaches 50 percent of the country's GDP with the output of the state-owned enterprises (SOEs) shrinking to one-third.

On its own, the world's changing economic landscape, particularly in China, is certain to have a swift and meaningful impact on investors. But when we consider how the forces of technology will amplify and accelerate this impact, the results become even more dramatic. Specifically, the impending ubiquity of the Internet will profoundly increase the rate at which economic power is redistributed. Remember the equation, $D = RT$? In junior high, most of us were taught that this meant distance (D) equals the rate (R) of travel multiplied by the time (T) spent traveling. By transposing the variables, we can determine T by dividing D by R. Therefore, time is distance traveled divided by speed of travel.

Now let us add to this equation the variable of the Internet, which allows information to travel at instantaneous speeds. In doing so, we discover that, with the Internet as our informational conduit, distance no longer matters as it once did. China is now our virtual next door neighbor, and the impact of its growth will be quicker and more keenly felt than we ever thought possible. Time and distance are being negated and the globe is becoming a single community in which change is the only certainty.

All of this points to a gigantic paradigm shift within the world economy. For the U.S. equity markets, this paradigm shift, which will be largely driven by China's impending dominance, may be as disruptive as it is rapid. Indeed, from the statistics presented earlier, it would appear that China's growing "star power" on the world stage is all but unstoppable. In some respects, it is. But there are certain characteristics of the Chinese economy that are both hindering its growth and increasing its dependence on other dominant countries, such as the United States.

One of the constraints to China's growth is the global shortage of industrial commodities, including the limits of the country's own natural resources. Since 2001, for example, Chinese imports of oil have risen by about 40 percent. In the long run, Chinese oil consumption will certainly continue to increase, though probably not at quite this magnitude.[10] A more realistic estimate would have total oil consumption by all Asian countries, including China, rising by about 8 percent annually. Even so, this 8 percent yearly increase would still call for daily Asian oil consumption to double from 20 million barrels to 40 million barrels in less than 10 years. This is a very striking increase, especially when we note that total global oil production presently averages over 81 million barrels per day.[11]

In addition to its growing demand for oil, China also faces the problem of water contamination, which now threatens to put the brakes on certain segments of the country's economy. In China, the amount of potable water per capita is only one-fourth of that in the United States. Combined with the water dilemma is the fact that agricultural land is shrinking and the Chinese are eating more meat-based products, which is a less efficient means of obtaining nutrition from the land than the traditional Chinese diet of mainly rice, grains, and vegetables. Taken together, the lack of potable water and the changes in the land's agricultural makeup will certainly impact the national economy, but could also undermine the health and well-being of the country's growing labor force.

This brings us to what is, in our opinion, the biggest problem currently faced by China. China's boom is not underpinned by *consumption.* Rather, the country's extreme recent growth has been made possible by *investment,* illustrated by the fact that nearly 50 percent of its GDP is comprised of investment spending. When China becomes unable to sustain growth through investment spending alone, growth rates will decline. This decline appears especially possible when we consider that the marginal efficiency of capital deployed in China is likely falling as we write. If growth drops below 7 percent per annum, it will lead to rising unemployment and will cause corporate profitability to plummet. Because of this, China needs to create 20 million new jobs per year to absorb the job losses occurring within the state-owned enterprises, which are estimated to equal 8 million per year.

With this in mind, let's take a look at the composition of the Chinese workforce. China's population is 1.3 billion, around 900 million of which may be assumed to be of working age. Let's also assume a labor participation rate of 65 percent. Given that an industrializing economy normally requires 20 percent of its workforce to be employed in manufacturing, this raises the prospect of manufacturing employment in China to 120 million workers. This is a staggering total when we consider that for all the Organization for Economic Cooperation and Development (OECD) countries combined, there are only 80 million workers employed in manufacturing. In our view, this is the clearest possible evidence of Freeman's "positive supply-side shock" to the global labor market.

So, in summary, the continuation of China's tremendous recent growth is currently under attack by a glut of labor and the menace of unemployment. How, then, is China protecting itself from these threats to its advancement within the global economy? We believe that the answer lies in a M.A.D policy between China and the United States.

China and the United States—A M.A.D. Policy

M.A.D. stands for Mutually Assured Destruction. During the Cold War, a M.A.D. policy developed between the United States and the United Soviet Socialist Republic. The basic premise of this policy was a tit-for-tat approach to nuclear warfare: "If you launch a nuclear missile, we will respond with a launch of our own. No one wins and everyone loses."

Today, it can be said that the United States and China have a similar policy in place, except that it is an economic one. The United States buys China's goods and China buys our Treasury Bonds and Agency paper. If one party stops playing its role, the other will stop as well, and economic growth will come to a standstill. The dollar will decline in value, interest rates will rise, and a recession, or worse, could be in the cards for the United States and the world at large. For China's government, the outlook would be particularly catastrophic, as the resulting rise in unemployment would lead to widespread dissatisfaction with the current regime.

To further explain why China has elected to maintain this M.A.D. economic policy with the United States, let's revisit a point in our nation's history when Americans were facing unemployment problems similar to those of the Chinese. In Chapter 2, we discussed the passage of the Full Employment Act of 1946. This law had three objectives. Our government and related institutions, the Fed, and the U.S. Treasury, were (1) to pursue growth of national output at a rate consistent with (2) full employment and (3) stable prices. For the most part, we achieved two out of three goals. Over the ensuing 20 years, growth was solid and employment rose as a result of a huge pent-up demand for consumer goods and services following the war. This growth in national output and employment was also fueled by the large saving pools that existed at the consumer level. But, while this law was successful in stimulating real economic growth, inflation went through the roof. Reflecting this inflation, interest rates rose dramatically from just over 2 percent to 14 percent in the years between 1945 and the early 1980s. However, because the Full Employment Act was really about employment at any cost, it is fair to say that the law's primary underlying intention was fulfilled, even though not all of its stated objectives were met.

In some respects, China's decision to tie its currency to the U.S. dollar in 1995 and its accession to WTO membership in December of 2001 placed the country in a position similar to the United States in 1946. Much like the motivation behind the Full Employment Act, China's decision to peg its currency and join the WTO was all about employment.

As discussed in prior pages, China's demographics are changing rapidly, and this will have an enormous impact on the country's employment profile. For instance, 200 million people are in the process of moving from the country to the cities, and this migration is transforming the makeup of China's urban workforce. In addition, China's SOEs are entities that "employ" people but add little value to the country's GDP. In the end, China must find ways to employ its growing urban labor pool in real jobs that translate into real growth and, to do so, it will gladly run the risk of inflation and excess investment through foreign capital deployment.

In the middle of the twentieth century, unemployment was the United States' social nightmare, and now, at the start of the twenty-first century, it is China's. In order to ensure that this nightmare does not become a waking reality, China has joined with the United States to pursue a new version of the M.A.D. policy.

At the same time, as pointed out by the *Economist,* China's ability to produce goods more cheaply has pushed down the prices of many goods around the world. In America, for example, the average prices of shoes and clothing have fallen by 10 percent in the past decade, a drop of 35 percent in real terms. So, in many ways, the current M.A.D. policy between the United States and China has done what the United States was unable to do in 1946—spur national growth, increase employment, and keep inflation under control all at the same time.

Therefore, the M.A.D. economic policy between the United States and China is working. Both nations need one another. China needs employment opportunities, which the United States fulfills by an ongoing demand for Chinese goods, and the United States needs financing to manage its trade and fiscal deficits, which China fulfills by investing in U.S. Treasury bonds. This policy may not be stable in the long run, but it appears to be a functioning paradigm that will stay in place for the foreseeable future.

Many investment theorists have already developed models of how this M.A.D. policy functions. For many, the question at hand is why emerging countries like China prefer to invest in relatively low-yielding U.S. Treasury bonds when, all things considered, they could realize a higher return by investing in their own economies. One explanation is provided by the "Bretton Woods 2" thesis developed by Michael Dooley, David Folkerts-Landau, and Peter Garber at Deutsche Bank. In this model, Asian economies have deliberately undervalued their currency in order to maintain a high export level and therefore maintain employment growth. As the theory goes, this purposeful undervaluation is achieved by the purchase of U.S. Treasuries.[12]

Whatever the specific mechanics of its underlying cause, the M.A.D. policy offers us a larger lesson; all things considered, globalization is a good thing and has been rewarding for both citizens and investors throughout the world. The Law of Comparative Advantage, in which every nation specializes in making what it makes well and then trading those goods for other goods and services it desires, is the "unseen hand" that allows everyone to prosper. Over the next 10 years, the most important function of our international economy will be to refine the trading paradigm between the developing countries that offer labor and low wages, and the developed countries that possess capital and technology. The current M.A.D. policy is helping to realize the benefits of this system, and the world's inhabitants are better off because of it.

But there is an important and somewhat unsettling question that results from our discussion of the Chinese/American M.A.D. policy. Specifically, what is the near-term effect of this policy on the financial stability of the United States?

The De Facto Dollar Zone

When one refers to the current state of U.S. finances, it is hard not to think of our deficits. Throughout recent economic history, much has been made of the twin deficits of the United States. And considering the aforementioned fact that many countries, such as China, continue to invest in dollar-denominated securities, what sort of danger do our deficits pose to the stability of the global economy? In other words, if our deficits are such a problem, why have countries not abandoned dollar assets and why are our interest rates still relatively low?

Perhaps the answer lies in a different application of the Law of Comparative Advantage. We believe that, through the pegging of currencies to the dollar, a broader definition of the word "nation" is unfolding—one based not on geography but, rather, on the existence of a shared currency. Because of this currency-based linkage, the allocation of dollar assets can work in much the same manner as the food/clothing paradigm that was presented earlier in this chapter.

Presently, China and other Asian countries are sending far more capital to the United States than is needed to finance the U.S. trade deficit. Based on net capital inflows in 2003 and 2004, the amount of this foreign capital was about one-third more than necessary. These capital inflows and the corresponding shifts in trade patterns are occurring under nearly uniform monetary conditions and, as such, are the mirror images of resource reallocations or changing divisions of labor within a single currency system. (Again, recall the food/clothing paradigm.) Because this single currency system can be governed by the Law of Comparative Advantage, one can see how a de facto "dollar zone" could encompass countries such as China, Hong Kong, Taiwan, Malaysia, Singapore, Thailand, South Korea, Japan, and, of course, the United States. In 2005, the combined GDP of this group was $21 trillion with a 5.27 percent growth rate.[13] This group's exports account for approximately 45 percent of the world's exports and 50 percent of its imports.

Now, let's see what the formation of this dollar zone means for the state of U.S. finances, specifically where our deficits are concerned. In aggregate, the dollar zone's trade deficit with the rest of the world was $325 billion in 2004. The United States accounted for about $300 billion and the remaining $25 billion was attributed to the Asian members of the zone. The total $325 billion deficit was 1.7 percent of the dollar zone's combined GDP. And if the North American Free Trade Agreement (NAFTA) and the Organization of the Petroleum Exporting Countries (OPEC) were included in a somewhat looser definition of a dollar zone, then the corresponding increase in total GDP would make the deficit disappear.

To better explain this line of reasoning, it's helpful to recall the arguments from the Reagan administration about the deficit. The idea was that the deficit was not a problem because we owed the money to ourselves. The debt of the Federal government was owned by its citizens and therefore it did not matter to us—sort of like having the left pocket of our pants empty of money but the right pocket full.* If we extend that concept to the dollar zone members, it leads us to the view that these deficits of ours matter much less than many pundits believe.

This is why China and other countries continue to be comfortable pursuing a M.A.D. economic policy with the United States: because much of our world is now encompassed by a dollar zone that is governed by the Law of Comparative Advantage and, therefore, reduces the danger of deficit formation.

Admittedly, the manner in which this dollar zone functions is a hypothesis at best. However, if this hypothesis has validity, interest rates should be lower than what they otherwise would be, productivity should be better than expected, and so should corporate profits. In other words, globalization improves the economic characteristics of the international marketplace. But, to make it all work requires that a rule of law be accepted by all parties. Much of this law is spelled out in the WTO's charter for its members that now includes China.

In fact, China's decision to accept the strict conditions of its WTO accession is a powerful indication of a worldwide willingness to play by the aforementioned "rule of law" that enables the maintenance of the de facto dollar zone. Nicholas Lardy describes this eloquently in his book, *Integrating China into the Global Economy*. In this book, Lardy points out that

---

*There was a "crowding out" argument at the time dealing with the deficit's impact on interest rates, but it could never be proven satisfactorily.

China's requirements for WTO membership were severe to the point of being discriminatory. In fact, the protocols to which China was forced to comply were far more burdensome than those experienced by any other member nation. Yet, despite the harsh nature of these accession requirements, China agreed to meet almost all demands put forth by the WTO.[14]

As Lardy states, China's willingness to abide by WTO standards is evidence of the intensity of the country's desire to be a part of the global economy. Through China's actions, we can infer that the implementation of a "rule of law" throughout the global marketplace is a real possibility. As such, the American/Chinese M.A.D. policy and the de facto dollar zone may be functional paradigms for some time yet.

The Floating Dollar

While we continue to have faith in how the de facto dollar zone will function within our new borderless marketplace, it would be irresponsible to ignore the potential dangers of this scenario. We believe the floating dollar is among the most prominent of these dangers.

The problem with the floating dollar is that its hegemony allows the major players in the world economy to act in ways that may initially appear beneficial to national self-interest. But, when viewed under a wider, multinational lens, the behavior of these individual nations, who are all operating under dollar-based currencies, are fundamentally illogical and potentially irresponsible.

As Clyde Prestowitz points out in his book, *Three Billion New Capitalists:* "Americans consume too much and save too little while Asians save too much and consume too little. Some are playing a mercantilist . . . game while others are playing more or less free trade and open markets. Yet, all are pretending that all are playing the free trade game."[15]

Prestowitz's essential question is one that we presented in the prior section: Can trading partners of the United States really be happy with a reserve currency they have to earn while we simply have to print it? In order for a satisfactory currency equilibrium to be maintained, there has to be a certain amount of faith placed in the United States with regard to its policy toward the dollar. So far, we have been able to avoid major international disagreements on this front, and the de facto dollar zone has remained more or less intact. But, the world is changing and so is our country's continued ability to control the value of the dollar in our favor. So what will happen when the tides turn and we can no longer win the "fair" way by strengthening the dollar through competitive behavior? Will we simply print money and inflate away the liabilities? These are complex questions with complex answers. But one thing is abundantly clear: when the economic interests of dollar-reliant nations are disparate, the potential for misunderstanding and conflict is enormous. Therefore, it is easy to imagine how complications surrounding the floating dollar could have an unfavorable effect on future equity returns. In the next chapter, we will see how a slowdown in U.S. consumer spending could also affect both the value of the dollar and the stability of the de facto dollar zone.

Dollar Devaluation

Dollar devaluation is, in our mind, another threat to the ongoing stability of the de facto dollar zone.

Dollar devaluation is already underway and may continue by another 20 percent. If this level of devaluation is reached, the global capital/labor interrelationship will be poised for yet another change. If the dollar declines in value, the Law of Comparative Advantage could generate an industrial renaissance in the United States, in which the American labor force will once again be put to work in manufacturing industries. However, we believe that this partial switch back to a manufacturing-based economy will be relatively modest given the fact that much of our country's manufacturing capacity is currently eroded beyond reusability.

As for the "capital" side of the equation, financial power will shift to the countries that have the largest proportion of stockholders' equity denominated in the strengthening currencies. In takeover terms, these countries will cease being the hunted and will become the hunters. As a result, foreign-based manufacturers may well become the acquirers in the reindustrialization of America once the dollar has fallen an appropriate amount.

As previously discussed, the United States has recently engaged in monetary and fiscal expansionary policies unseen since World War II. Our twin deficits of trade and treasury exceed a combined $1 trillion, 85 percent of which has been borrowed from the rest of the world. In some ways, the dangers of these gigantic deficits are mitigated by the emergence of a de facto dollar zone. It is possible, however, to envision a scenario in which the magnitude of these debts becomes unsustainable and will result in a devaluation of our currency. Over the next several years, it is likely that the U.S. dollar could show signs of troubling deterioration, which could once again shift the equilibrium of the international economy.

Conclusion

Globalization is today's dominant investment paradigm, and it is characterized by some remarkable new realities. Three billion people are entering the global economy and they all want better lives and higher living standards; international media outlets have spread the values of Western-style capitalism to nearly every corner of the globe; and the wiring and interconnection of the world through the Internet will only happen once and it is happening now at a phenomenal speed. Taken together, there is a global contagion of economic wisdom: an understanding by leaders the world over that economic growth is necessary for political survival. In order to lure foreign direct investment and encourage a wider distribution of wealth, these leaders are instituting policies of lower taxes, less regulation, increased technological innovation, expanded credit availability, improved educational opportunities, institutionalization of property rights, and deregulation.

The state of global growth currently reflects these positive occurrences. According to the *Economist,* the world is currently in the most synchronized expansion since the late 1980s, with over 60 percent of global GDP increasing at a faster rate than that of the United States. Recently, world industrial production has been rising at nearly 5 percent year over year, almost equal to that of last year and almost double that of 2004. In the fall of 2006, the IMF once again increased its forecast for global growth in 2007 from 4.7 percent to 4.9 percent, which would make 2007 the record fifth consecutive year of global growth expansion. Furthermore, the *Economist* reported in 2005 that world GDP growth was tracking at its fastest rate in nearly 30 years. For the second time since at least 1980 (the first time was in 2004), all 55 countries followed by the magazine were growing, and some 60 percent of monitored emerging markets were expanding at 6 percent or more.

Simply put, globalization is producing some dramatically positive results. And these results directly support the value of a Shareholder Yield-based approach to investing. Because of the labor arbitrage efficiencies made possible by the Law of Comparative Advantage, global labor costs are lower on aggregate, which has resulted in higher global free cash flow. As the world's factory floor is being rewired through globalization, more goods and services are being created per unit of resources, which means that more resources (i.e., free cash flow) can be deployed in a manner that directly enhances shareholder value through dividends, share buybacks, and debt reduction.

In the next chapter, we continue our discussion of the changing investment landscape by discussing several other current trends that, in addition to an understanding of the forces of globalization, are crucial to the development of an effective investment strategy.

CHAPTER 6

Interest Rates, Bubbles, and Punctuated Equilibriums

As any savvy investor knows, there are few things that matter in finance more than interest rates. Interest rates are the dominant component of the discount rate for virtually all investments, they provide the key metric when valuing public securities, and they serve as the primary denominator in the present value mechanism that discounts the future streams of benefits to the holders of public securities.

The recognition of the crucial role played by interest rates is an essential component of a successful investment philosophy. We have already spent a great deal of time discussing how the movement of interest rates has colored our view of the capital markets. In Part One, for instance, we discussed how climbing interest rates lead to falling P/Es, which in turn allow the three components of Shareholder Yield—cash dividends, share repurchase, and debt paydowns—to eclipse the P/E ratio as dominant positive explanatory variables in equity market returns. Then, in the first chapter of Part Two, we explained how coordinated expansionary monetary policies kept interest rates lower than they would have been otherwise and allowed the forces of globalization to gather momentum and to aid the creation of a de facto dollar zone.

In Chapter 6, we resume our discussion of interest rates and their effect on the investment landscape by reviewing several of the potential dangers of rising interest rates. We believe that, while higher interest rates will certainly open up new opportunities for the informed investor via the application of the Shareholder Yield philosophy, we are also certain that many new dangers and pitfalls will be manufactured as a result of the Fed's return to a contraction-oriented monetary policy. These pitfalls may include (and, in some cases, already have included) the deflation of several of the economic bubbles that have recently hovered over the investment landscape. Rising interest rates will instigate the puncture of three bubbles: (1) the housing bubble, (2) the liquidity bubble, and (3) the corporate profit bubble. This chapter is dedicated to exploring how these scenarios will unfold and how the behavior of the equity markets could change as a result.

Punctuated Equilibrium

Before we move on to the specifics of each imperiled bubble, it will be useful to discuss the manner in which their destruction could impact the marketplace. To do so, we will look beyond the world of finance. Sometimes, to gain fresh insights into the dynamics of investing, it is valuable to consider how ideas from diverse schools of thought can help us see the capital markets in a new and compelling light. In that spirit, we'd like to discuss the concept of *punctuated equilibrium* and the manner in which this theory of evolutionary biology can be applied to today's financial landscape.

The theory of punctuated equilibrium was developed by Stephen Jay Gould, the highly regarded professor of paleontology, biology, and natural history at Harvard University. Punctuated equilibrium describes a new understanding of Darwinian evolutionism in which species evolve not through slow, gradual genetic modifications but, rather, through intermittent periods of sudden and rapid change. Gould asserted that, when evolution does occur, it happens sporadically and occurs relatively quickly compared to a species' full duration on earth.

We believe the theory of punctuated equilibrium is remarkably applicable to the world of investing, especially as we find ourselves on the edge of tomorrow's new economic paradigms. Sudden equilibrium shifts do not only occur within fossil records: they occur within securities markets as well. Such shifts occur because of changes in key variables such as real economic growth, inflation, interest rates, productivity, and profits. Our investment landscape has already been suddenly and dramatically altered by changes to these variables, and we will show why the immediate future may follow a similar path. In the remainder of this chapter, we explore how one of these key variables—the interest rate—will punctuate our financial equilibrium by either accelerating, initiating, or predicting the deflation of the three aforementioned bubbles in housing, liquidity, and corporate profits.

The Next Punctuation—Interest Rates

Globalization, as discussed in the previous chapter, is the financial world's most recent and possibly most dramatic instance of "punctuation." Because of the sudden labor/wage arbitrage possibilities inherent in the Law of Comparative Advantage, international productivity and profits have surged, and gross domestic products (GDPs) in the G-7 countries have reached record highs.

Now, we are on the cusp of another punctuation, the results of which could be a great deal more negative than the changes brought about by globalization. To fully understand why our investment landscape could be headed toward another instance of punctuated equilibrium, it is first necessary to review the relationship between the real economy and the financial economy.

In Chapter 2, we presented a schematic for explaining how what happens in the real economy drives the financial economy (Figure 2.3). To remind ourselves of how the model works, let's plug in some numbers. Over very long periods of time, real GDP growth has averaged around 3 percent, a percentage that has recently been positively influenced by the effects of globalization. Coincidentally, inflation has averaged around 3 percent as well, albeit with much wider period-to-period swings (from negative numbers to positive double digits). Therefore, if we combine real GDP growth with inflation, we find that nominal GDP has grown around 6 percent over much of economic history. As we know from our discussion in Part One, growth in corporate profits (EPS) has mirrored nominal GDP growth over time.

Later in this chapter, when we discuss the likelihood of the decline of the corporate profit bubble, we will present a series of equations that further explicate this link between GDP and corporate profits. But, for now, let's stick to the topic of interest rates. Because the crux of this chapter is an analysis of how changing interest rates can affect the global economic condition, it's important to revisit the manner in which interest rates fit into our model of the real and financial economies. Interest rates fit into this model by way of the P/E ratio. These ratios have historically fluctuated with interest rates and inflation in an inverse fashion, as shown earlier in Figure 2.5.

With this in mind, let's fast forward our model of the real/financial economies to the present era. In recent years, much of the activity in the real/financial economies has been driven by concerns over the "inflation" aspect of the equation, as you may recall from our discussion in Chapter 2. Specifically, the world's monetary authorities (led by our Fed) feared deflation as the aftermath of the equity bubble implosion in 2000. As a result, interest rates were lowered in order to encourage investment both in the public and private markets. With declining discount rates applied to investment options, the present value of those options increased greatly and investors became far less risk averse than in earlier days. In fact, the riskier the investment, the better. As a result, investors began an aggressive international hunt for yield, inflating asset prices and exacerbating the global financial imbalance. In addition, the low rates maintained by the central banks created one of the world's great "carry trades" in which investors, particularly hedge funds, could borrow short and lend long in order to capture the spread in interest rates and duration. In many ways, the popularity of these carry trades fueled the economic bubbles that this chapter is dedicated to discussing.

However, the days of persistently low interest rates (and the carry trades that resulted from them) appear to have ended. The world's central banks have changed their tune. Just as they had once loosened their monetary policies in tandem, they are now engaged in joint tightening. As we've mentioned several times before, there is no financial variable more powerful than interest rates. Therefore, it comes with no small consequence that our Fed has raised short-term interest rates 17 times in the past few years. To understand the effects of this profound transition in monetary policy, we need only compare the current interest rate curve with that of one year ago (see Figure 6.1).

The upward shift and overall flattening of today's interest rate curve has put an end to the carry trade and has reduced the present value of investments made as recently as two years ago. The world's central bankers are raising the cost of capital

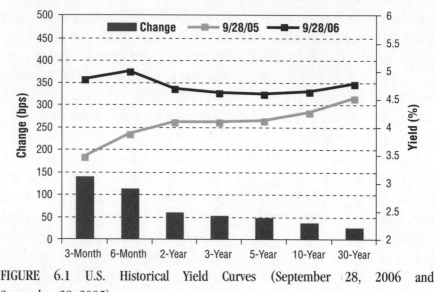

FIGURE 6.1 U.S. Historical Yield Curves (September 28, 2006 and September 28, 2005)

Source: Bloomberg LP.

and the resulting effects are rippling through the financial markets. Record compressed spreads in the bond market are about to widen, and the risk reduction trade is on in earnest. (As a result, look out for more than one hedge fund to go under.) This is a strong indication that we may be witnessing the early stages of a transition to another equilibrium.

In our view, this new equilibrium will largely be characterized by the deflation of three major economic bubbles: the housing bubble, the liquidity bubble, and the corporate profit bubble. The rest of this chapter is dedicated to discussing these bubbles in detail and explaining how their demise could result in a sudden equilibrium shift.

Section One: The Housing Bubble

Like the concept of globalization, much has recently been made of the housing bubble and its impending burst. By all accounts, the housing market has already begun its inevitable decline, even in parts of our country that were once thought immune to a dramatic softening of housing prices. As investors, our goal is to not only understand the changes that are taking place in the housing sector, but to capture the present and future implications to the capital markets and to the economy as a whole.

The Birth of the Housing Bubble

Given the title of this chapter, it will come as no surprise that we have linked the popping of the housing bubble to the rise in interest rates. This is a logical assumption because it was the persistence of low interest rates, after all, that led to the creation of this bubble in the first place. Specifically, we attribute the birth of the housing bubble to three interrelated concepts: (1) low interest rates, (2) creative financing strategies, and (3) the creation of systemic risk through securitization.

While low interest rates have certainly resulted in several positive economic trends (as outlined elsewhere in this book), they have also contributed to the housing bubble because they have provided an incentive for homeowners to borrow cash to purchase homes as investment vehicles. In fact, according to the National Association of Realtors, 27.7 percent of all houses purchased in 2005 were for investment purposes, not owner occupation. Another 12 percent were bought as vacation homes. Low interest rates, coupled with riskier forms of mortgage finance, allowed these buyers to borrow more and more in order to finance their investments in housing. In fact, the recent housing finance environment was so attractive that over 40 percent of all first-time buyers and 25 percent of all buyers made no down payment on their home mortgage last year. Adjustable rate mortgages (ARMs) have risen to 50 percent of all mortgages in those states with the biggest housing price increases. In today's world, little or no documentation of a borrower's assets, employment, or income is required for a loan. When getting a loan is this easy, and when interest rates are this attractive, the housing market bubble cannot help but grow dangerously out of proportion.

As alluded to in the prior paragraph, low interest rates led to investments in the housing market that were speculative and potentially irresponsible. What's more, many of these investments were underpinned by radically creative and complex financing structures, a phenomenon that both helped the housing bubble grow and contributed to its fundamental instability. The popularity of these financing structures is largely the result of the policies put in place by Alan Greenspan, the former chairman of the Fed. A serial bubble blower, his policies first created a bubble in the equity markets that was then transitioned to the housing market. The bursting of the equity bubble at the beginning of this century had extremely negative consequences for the health of our nation's economy, but it is nothing compared to the financial fall-out that may occur when the housing bubble is punctured.

Bubbles are caused, in part, by the widespread acceptance of irresponsible financing strategies, and the housing bubble began when Greenspan provided negative real rates of interest as a method of offsetting deflation. This strategy may have once worked in Japan but, in the United States, it led to the creation of the biggest housing bubble in centuries. Because of the Fed's insistence on exceptionally low interest rates, we have gone from "my house is my castle" to "my house is my ATM machine." This goes a long way toward explaining how, over the past several years, the American consumer has consistently spent more than he has made.

Let us further examine the phenomenon of creative financing that was instigated by Greenspan's persistently low interest rates. The following facts are courtesy of Lon Witter of Witter & Westlake Investments in Louisville, Kentucky:

- Nearly one-third of new mortgages and home equity loans in 2005 were interest-only, compared to 0.6 percent in 2000.
- 43 percent of first-time home buyers in 2005 put no money down.
- More than 15 percent of home buyers in 2005 owe at least 10 percent more than their homes are worth.
- 10 percent of all home owners with mortgages have no equity in their home.
- More than $2.7 trillion in mortgage loans will adjust to higher rates in 2007.

We can use the fifth and final statistic to get a sense of the real impact of these creative financing strategies on the average home owner. As Witter states, let's assume that the homeowner has a $250,000 three-year adjustable-rate mortgage with an annual 2 percent rate hike cap. If the monthly payment is $1,123 today, the monthly payment will jump to $1,419 with the first adjustment and to $1,748 with the second adjustment. That is a $7,500 per year rise in mortgage costs to maintain the same mortgage. Even worse, this comes at a time when median incomes in the United States are stagnant or rising little.

Historical precedent tells us that financing schemes such as the one outlined here come with dire consequences. One example is the junk bond situation in the late 1980s. If you were the acquirer, the concept was to use the target's balance sheet as collateral for whatever debt you incurred to enable the takeover offer in the first place. If this sounds like the same strategy employed by W.E.S.Ray in its acquisition of Gibson Greeting Cards, it is no coincidence. It *is* the same strategy but, in the junk bond scenario, it was taken to irresponsible extremes. Remember United Airlines and the effort mounted to take it private? As many of us remember, that game ended in 1989 with the mini market crash started by the collapse of this deal.

Recently, however, this same scheme has allowed millions of prospective home buyers to buy homes with little or no money down, with the homes to be acquired as collateral. But what happens if the value of the homes falls, as is happening now? At some point, the home owner walks, leaving the mortgage lender with the house. So far, the mortgage lenders' response to this has been simple: they have floated the loan.

But the mortgage lenders' response is what has made the bursting of the housing bubble an event of national concern. The mortgage lenders have securitized these unpaid housing loans. Through the process of securitization, they have taken local risks, aggregated them, and turned them into national, systemic risks. It is *systemic* risk that is at the heart of every bubble, not *specific* risk, and the process of securitization, which was made possible by low interest rates and creative financing options, has increased our economy's exposure to housing-related systemic risk. For developed countries, capital markets are liquid and deep enough to handle almost any specific risk. It is only when an entire asset class is at risk that the system is placed in harm's way. This is where housing is today—trapped in a bubble of unsustainably high prices and perilous systemic risk. Like junk bonds in the 1980s, this structure will collapse when collateral values fall below asset values and stay there for a while. The mortgage institution has granted the homeowner a "put": the ability to walk away from the loan obligation when the gap between realized value and the mortgage payable becomes large enough to warrant such an action. When this happens *en masse,* the housing bubble will burst in its entirety, the consequences will be nationwide, and the equity markets will decline.

The Magnitude of the Housing Bubble

Before we take a closer look at what will happen when the bubble bursts, it will be useful to quantify the size of the bubble itself. So, just how big is this housing bubble? By all accounts, it is incredibly large. In fact, according to the *Economist,* the "worldwide rise in house prices is the biggest bubble in history." The *Economist*'s argument runs as follows: "The total value of residential property in developed economies rose by more than $30 trillion over the past five years to over $75 trillion, an increase equivalent to 100 percent of these countries' comprised GDPs." This massive increase in the value of residential property leads us to believe that house prices are greatly overvalued.

The most compelling evidence for this assertion is the diverging relationship between housing prices and rents. The ratio of housing prices to rents can be thought of as a P/E ratio of sorts for the housing market. This number has never been higher than it is today. In America, for example, our ratio of housing prices to rents is 35 percent higher than the average level for the period 1975 to 2000. This ratio is even higher in Britain, Australia, and Spain. In other words, the scale and scope of this housing bubble is truly daunting. To quote the *Economist* once again: "Prepare for the economic pain when [the bubble] pops."

The Popping Has Already Begun

As many investors are no doubt aware, the popping has already begun. This is most keenly evident in the decrease to house prices and the increase in the number of houses for sale and the length of time these houses have stayed on the market. Here are some statistics to help illustrate these points. In the United States, house prices have been falling since last summer (2005) and the stock of unsold homes has grown rapidly. According to the National Association of Home Builders, the number of homes for sale in 2005 was 19 percent higher than a year ago. On a year-over-year basis, which is the most accurate way to compare sales given seasonal disparities, new home sales in July 2006 were down 22 percent from July 2005. As of July 2006, the median price for a new home was $230,000, which represents an 11 percent decline from only three months earlier. Inventory of existing single-family homes has increased from a 4.5 month supply in July 2005 to a 7.2 month supply in July 2006. This represents the most months of supply for existing single-family homes on the market since July 1997. This change in supply/demand is aggravated by rising mortgage rates. According to Freddie Mac, the 30-year fixed-rate mortgage in September 2006 was around 6.40 percent versus 5.77 percent a year ago.

The bubble is also starting to burst on the "lender" side of the equation. As quoted earlier, Lon Witter made this important point in his *Barron's* editorial by citing the example of Washington Mutual (WaMu). At the end of 2003, only 1 percent of Washington Mutual's option ARMs were considered negative amortization loans.* However, just one year later, 21 percent of WaMu's option ARMs were in negative amortization and, another year later, the percentage had ballooned to 47

---

*Negative amortization is a cockamamie accounting procedure that allows the lender to book interest owed from the mortgage but not yet received in cash as income with the same amount added to the principal mortgage owed to the bank. The accounting entry is a debit to loan and credit to mortgage income, even when no cash has actually changed hands.

percent. In terms of the overall value of loans outstanding, the percentage in negative amortization was 55 percent. With the endorsement of GAAP, in the first quarter of 2005, WaMu booked $25 million of negative amortization as earnings and, in the first quarter of 2006, that number had increased eight-fold to $203 million.

Taken together, the decrease in average house prices, the growing number of houses on the market (plus the extended amount of time they stay there), and the imperiled finances of many mortgage lenders point to the fact that the bursting of the housing bubble is already well underway.

The Post-Bubble Economy

So what will our economy look like once the housing bubble bursts in earnest? First of all, since much of our country's recent GDP growth has been financed by "cash-out" mortgages, GDP growth rates will decline when housing equity withdrawals start to decelerate. Over the past several years, housing equity withdrawals have been massive, but have already begun to slow sharply, which will cause household spending to stagnate as a consequence.

For the United States, this trend is particularly significant. Goldman Sachs estimated that total housing-related equity withdrawals accounted for 7.4 percent of personal disposable income in 2004. Housing equity withdrawals are, therefore, a massive contributor to spending in the United States. Independent of any other world issues (China, Iraq, the fiscal and trade deficits, etc.) a decrease in housing equity would result in a meaningful slowing of economic growth and would contribute to declines in corporate profit growth rates. If we also consider a possible slowdown in China, which will result from the slowdown in the United States plus the anticipated decline in the marginal efficiency of capital deployed in China, the picture looks increasingly problematic for corporate profit growth. (Recall our discussion of the American/Chinese M.A.D. policy in Chapter 5.)

Furthermore, it is important to note that homes remain very expensive in relation to incomes. All things considered, we believe the most significant effect of the global liquidity boom for consumers over the past decade has been the rising property price to income ratio. If this ratio were to fall back down to its 1996 level, the global economy could easily suffer a recession. And because the housing bubble is beginning to burst in virtually every area of the country, we will soon witness the widespread demise of the consumer's "home ATM machine," which will do much to temper the exuberance of U.S. consumers.

Armed with these facts, it is easy to see how the bursting of the housing bubble may well result in deep and wide-ranging consequences. In fact, a study by the International Monetary Fund (IMF) found that output losses after house price busts in rich countries have, on average, been twice as large as those following crashes in stock markets. To make matters worse, crashes in the housing market are usually followed by recession. The reason that housing market crashes are able to wreak such economic havoc is the dual problem of unemployment and wealth destruction. For example, it is estimated that 40 percent of jobs created in America since 2001 have been in housing-related sectors such as construction, real estate lending, and brokering. In California, this problem is particularly apparent, as there was a registered broker for every house sold in the state in the year 2004. Therefore, it is easy to see how a precipitous decline in already-inflated house prices will have a massive effect on the employment status and wealth-generating potential of a huge portion of the labor pool. In fact, if we place the current market value of the U.S. housing stock at around $22 trillion, a 5 percent to 10 percent fall in housing prices would cause the net worth of American consumers to suffer a $1.1 trillion to $2.2 trillion decline.*

Going Out with a Bang, Not a Whimper

It is worth addressing those who might doubt the massive scale and scope of the housing bubble's puncture. Even though America's exposure to the collapse in housing prices seems unavoidable, there are those who cite the history of the American market and its resilience to housing busts to downplay this concern for the housing sector. After all, the United States was the only country to avoid a boom and bust during the 1970 to 2001 period studied by the IMF. In this study, the IMF looked at 14 countries and identified 20 housing "busts." A bust occurred when real prices, not nominal prices, fell. All but one of these 20 housing busts led to a recession, with GDP falling after three years to an average of 8 percent below its previous growth trend. In Japan, prices dropped for 14 years in a row, a 40 percent decrease from peak to trough.

Rather than supporting those who believe that real estate investments will decline modestly if at all, this historical data from the IMF, plus the unprecedented range and scale of the current housing bubble, point to the conclusion that the United States is much more vulnerable to a "bust" than in decades past. This time, the conditions are riskier, the stakes are higher, and it is very unlikely that the United States can continue to escape from housing bubbles unscathed.

In conclusion, today's investor cannot afford to ignore the dangers of the housing market bubble. This bubble has been created, in part, by the mixed blessing of low interest rates, and it will be punctured as interest rates rise. However, if we recognize the bubble's potential for changing the economic

---

* We are indebted to Rob Brown, Chief Investment Officer of Genworth Asset Management, for this example.

landscape, we can focus on companies and sectors that should continue to generate free cash flow, attract capital and perform well. Simply put, higher interest rates will cause this bubble to burst but the savvy investor need not go "bust."

Section Two: The Liquidity Bubble

The previous section explored how the economy's next instance of punctuated equilibrium could manifest itself in the form of a housing market decline. The next bubble under discussion—the liquidity bubble—is closely related to the housing market bubble. In fact, the liquidity bubble can be viewed as both the cause and the effect of the decline in residential asset values. In addition, the bursting of this bubble is also related to global financial imbalances and the dangers of hedge fund behavior. In our view, this phenomenon will occur hand-in-hand with rising interest rates and a growing risk-aversion on the part of investors and consumers. Let's take a look at how and why this complex scenario could take place.

Global Financial Imbalances

We believe the puncturing of the liquidity bubble could take the form of a global liquidity crisis in which the investment community as a whole will be forced to reevaluate its relationship to risk.* Before the recent contraction of worldwide monetary policy, low interest rates caused investors to seek out riskier investments in much the same way as it caused them to make irresponsible investments in the housing market. Now

---

*Before we outline the details of this argument, it is important to acknowledge that many of the ideas in this section are extensions of the issues raised in the European Central Bank's "Financial Stability Review" from June 2006. Unless otherwise footnoted, the quotes in this section have been excerpted from the "Financial Stability Review."

that the central banks have agreed to raise the cost of capital, investors have started to reevaluate their appetite for risk. In the words of the European Central Bank: "the main source of vulnerability in the period ahead continues to centre upon concern that a global search for yield, which began in 2003, may have led investors . . . either to underestimate or to take on too much risk." And when people lose their appetite for risk, they often lose their appetite for consumption, which has immediate and meaningful effects on liquidity.

This brings us to what is, in our opinion, one of the most worrisome indications that we are headed for a major economic "punctuation." The international markets currently suffer from what the European Central Bank deems "global financial imbalances," in which the economic relationships between countries and marketplaces have become increasingly unsustainable. One of the primary causes of this unsustainability is the fact that the world's most powerful engine of consumption (i.e., the U.S. consumer) appears ready to stall.

Before we take a closer look at the evidence behind this slowdown in U.S. consumption, let's first discuss how and why these "global financial imbalances" occurred in the first place. As cited in the prior paragraph, many of these imbalances are rooted in the United States and represent significant vulnerability for global financial system stability. First of all, American households have been dis-saving in record numbers. In 2005, our country's households ran a combined deficit of $477 billion: by far the lowest savings rate since 1929, as shown in Figure 6.2.[1]

This has resulted in growing funding pressures on global capital markets. Furthermore, U.S. imports have grown to twice the size of exports, causing the current account deficit to grow to a record-breaking 6 percent of U.S. GDP in 2005. In addition, the foreign holdings of U.S. Treasuries have more than doubled over the past 10 years. Today, 50 percent of U.S. treasury securities are held by foreign owners (Figure 6.3 on p. 113).

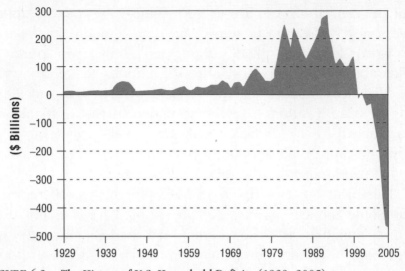

FIGURE 6.2   The History of U.S. Household Deficits (1929–2005)

Source: "Unlucky Ben Bernanke," *Grant's Interest Rate Observer,* vol. 24, no. 19 (October 6, 2006).

Based on the facts presented earlier, it is not hard to imagine how these global financial imbalances could unwind. If the United States becomes unable to finance its deficits, it could result in "an abrupt asset portfolio reallocation, either by the official or the private sector, or . . . a sudden deterioration in the risk appetite of global investors for accumulating U.S. securities in sufficiently large amounts." We are the reserve currency of the world; we can print dollars when all others must earn them. But, given our twin deficits and the severe imbalances in the international marketplace, how much longer can we expect international investors to remain confident in lending their money to the United States? In other words, if you owned our paper, how confident would you be that the United States would honor its debt obligations at the same level of purchasing power at which these debts were incurred? Why would the United States not allow inflation to resolve its debt obligations?

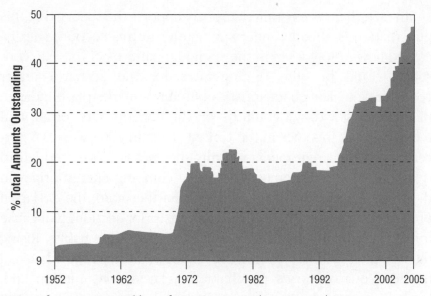

FIGURE 6.3   Foreign Holding of U.S. Treasuries (Q1 1952–Q4 2005, Percentage of Total Amounts Outstanding)

Source: U.S. Federal Reserve Board and European Central Bank Calculations.

Simply put: why trust us? As you may recall, several of these considerations—including the floating dollar and the de facto dollar zone—were previously discussed in Chapter 5.

If other nations do, in fact, stop trusting the economic hegemony of the United States, it could "entail sudden and destabilizing changes in global capital flow patterns." These sudden and destabilizing changes would include downward pressure on the U.S. dollar, further increases in interest rates, a cancellation of the American/Chinese M.A.D. policy, and, of course, the bursting of the liquidity bubble. And, because of the "increasingly global nature of the asset allocation process," these events would necessarily affect every aspect of the investment landscape. In our view, if this series of events comes to pass, a punctuation to our current equilibrium is nearly unavoidable.

In fact, there is existing data that supports the theory that this punctuation is already underway. Earlier in this section, we discussed how a slowdown in the spending patterns of the U.S. consumer could be the tripping wire for the scenario under consideration. The characteristics of today's marketplace indicate that such a slowdown could be on the horizon. First of all, real median family incomes in the United States in 2005 were 0.5 percent lower than real median family incomes in 2001.[2] Added to this stagnation in incomes are rapidly climbing energy prices in the form of gasoline and heating oil. Furthermore, the deflation of the housing market, as outlined in the prior section, will cause millions of Americans to reevaluate their spending habits. Rising interest rates will soon close the "home ATM machine" that had financed our country's penchant for excess consumption and, later this year, a huge volume of adjustable rate mortgages will require resets. All things considered, the outlook for discretionary spending cannot be good. Because U.S. consumer spending is equal to approximately 20 percent of world GDP, any modifications to our historical levels of consumption will necessarily impact every aspect of the international marketplace.

So, if this consumer spending slowdown indeed proves to be the case, what does it mean for the "feeder nations" that have benefited from the U.S. consumer? The answer is that these countries lack middle class populations large enough to generate sufficient internal demand. Put another way, when the United States stops buying, they will stop selling, creating a massive shift in the worldwide supply/demand paradigm. As discussed earlier, this could cause global financial imbalances to resolve themselves in a manner that destroys the liquidity bubble and creates the market's next big evolutionary event.

Hedge Funds

The imbalanced nature of global finances is only one of the drivers behind the upcoming liquidity-based equilibrium punctuation. There is also the disturbing presence of large, concentrated pools of capital that aggravate worldwide market volatility levels. Here, we're referring specifically to hedge funds.

Today, it is estimated by several sources that between 30 percent and 50 percent of the daily volume on the NYSE is from hedge funds. The popularity of these funds was driven in part by the low interest rate environment of prior years, in which investors sought out hedge funds in their search for return. As a product of the former liquidity bubble, we believe these funds possess certain characteristics that, as interest rates rise, may bode ill for the future of the investment landscape.

First of all, many of these funds have shown a troubling aversion to transparency standards. Even when the SEC sought minimum registration from these funds, many of them were able to avoid regulation in the form of extended lock-ups and other SEC disclosure conditions. On top of this, the current Fed chairman appears to hold the misguided opinion that self-regulation and market discipline is sufficient to keep hedge funds under control. Taken together, the magnitude of capital controlled by hedge funds, their often inconsistent adherence to best-practice standards, and the "blind-eye" policy of today's Federal Reserve sets the stage for yet another potential contribution to a punctuation within our economic equilibrium.

Let's take an even closer look at how the behavior of hedge funds could contribute to an upcoming global liquidity crisis. In recent years, hedge funds have been a large and growing presence in the credit risk transfer (CRT) market. During prior periods of lower interest rates and seemingly endless flows of global liquidity, investors sought outperformance by investing in high risk areas, such as the CRT market, thus potentially overpricing CRT products. As interest rates remained low and liquidity remained ample, the CRT market grew exponentially, largely as a result of hedge fund involvement. Now, however, as interest rates rise and the liquidity bubble begins to burst, the

CRT market (and, by extension, the hedge funds that invest in CRT products) appear particularly vulnerable and have become cause for legitimate concern. To quote the European Central Bank: "These concerns have included uncertainties about the obscure way in which these [CRT] markets have redistributed credit risks in the financial system and about the capability of these markets to function under stress, especially concerning the settlement of complex contractual arrangements."

In addition to their heavy involvement in the CRT market, hedge funds pose several other threats to the survival of the liquidity bubble. Specifically, hedge funds have placed the market in a precarious position because they have allowed large numbers of investors and large pools of capital to congregate within similar investment positions. To see why this is problematic, we can once again refer to evolutionary biology. When a certain habitat becomes overpopulated with any one species, the results on the ecosystem as a whole can be devastating and can often precipitate sudden and dramatic change. The same is true in the investment world; when too many investors become herded into the same investment positions (especially the high-risk positions favored by hedge funds), the stage is set for disaster. In the words of the European Central Bank: "Broad hedge fund investment strategies have . . . become increasingly correlated, thereby further increasing the potential adverse effects of disorderly exits from crowded trades." In fact, they note that "the correlation of hedge fund returns both within and across investment strategies [has now] surpassed levels seen just before the near-collapse of Long Term Capital Management in 1998." Furthermore, the European Central Bank cites these conditions as a potential threat to our market's equilibrium: "It is difficult to gauge what could cause correlated sell-offs and how damaging these could be, but one possible trigger could be an abrupt end of the recent global search for yield possibly induced by the tightening of global liquidity conditions."

At this point, it may be helpful to present some evidence for the assertion that the bursting of the liquidity bubble—or, in our chosen vernacular, the punctuation of the market equilibrium—is already being sensed by the investment community. In 2002 to 2004 and the first three quarters of 2005, hedge funds recorded net inflows that averaged an extremely robust $20 billion per quarter. However, in the final quarter of 2005, hedge funds recorded their first net outflows in several years, which alerted the managers of these funds to signs of trouble on the horizon.

In response to this, hedge funds have recently resorted to increasingly complex strategies designed to preserve their shrinking carry-trade premium and to lessen the potential of higher future outflows. In some funds, this has taken the form of investments in OTC derivatives and private equity-style investing. These strategies come with several key liquidity-related issues which some hedge funds have chosen to address by mechanisms such as "side pockets" and "side letters." Side pockets represent a separate class of capital in a hedge fund to account for illiquid holdings. According to the European Central Bank: "Sidepocketed assets usually do not earn performance fees and are nonredeemable until the assets are finally sold. However, in this way the returns on a fund's most volatile assets do not contribute to its returns, and can thereby dampen the overall volatility of hedge fund performance." Similarly, side letters are provisions that offer certain benefits to a hedge fund's largest investors. These benefits can include preferential withdrawal terms, early information on adverse fund developments, lower fees and other volume discounts. In addition to raising the obvious issues of transparency and informational equity, "such side letters also create a misleading impression of a fund's resilience to investor redemption."

So, does the presence of the strategies outlined in the prior paragraph serve as an indication that hedge funds have acknowledged the coming liquidity crisis? The answer is both yes and no. Yes, in the sense that hedge funds are clearly scrambling to reduce withdrawals based on liquidity concerns. However, there is also evidence that hedge funds have underestimated the magnitude of the coming punctuation. In support of this, the European Central Bank presents the results of a regression analysis in which hedge funds seem aware of potential dangers, yet unaware of their potential impact:

> All in all, the findings provide some support for the view that the hedge fund industry has benefited from the recent global search for yield, as aggregate net flows appear to be sensitive to investor risk appetite and to the level of short-term interest rates. This also raises the risk that hedge fund managers may have underestimated investor redemption risk arising from global financial conditions that is not so apparent at the level of individual hedge funds. An unexpected end of the recent global search for yield could cause investors to withdraw their money abruptly, thereby exerting funding liquidity pressures on individual hedge funds. This could trigger substantial share sell-offs and challenge perceptions regarding the degree of liquidity prevailing in affected markets.

In summary, we believe that hedge fund activity is poised to play a role in the capital market's next instance of punctuated equilibrium. Over the past several years, investors have been on an aggressive hunt for yield, which has led to increased hedge fund inflows. Now, however, it is clear that this same trend may have increased the market's vulnerability to risk reappraisal and abrupt asset price adjustments. In other words: "For financial markets, large and potentially correlated asset price adjustments could cause liquidity to dry up and undermine the hedging of financial risks." This means that hedge funds may cause the market equilibrium to be punctured sooner and more severely than many investors had anticipated.

The global liquidity bubble appears to be bursting, and it isn't difficult to see how this could result in another instance of punctuated equilibrium. From the presence of global financial imbalances to the dangerous role played by hedge funds, the international markets seem poised on the brink of rapid and destabilizing change. As in the case of the housing bubble, both the cause of the liquidity bubble's creation and the mechanism behind its decline is the interest rate.

Section Three: The Corporate Profit Bubble

The third and final bubble under analysis in this chapter is the corporate profit bubble. Over the past five years, corporate profits have shown remarkable rates of growth which have far exceeded the rate of growth of GDP. Much of this growth in profits reflects the enduring benefits of globalization and the labor/capital shift, as discussed in Chapter 5. But a portion of this growth reflects the influence of what we refer to as "temporary accelerants." These temporary accelerants, including low interest rates, have contributed to the creation of an unsustainable growth rate in corporate profits. Over the next several quarters, should interest rates remain at present levels or rise, this bubble could burst and current market levels will be faced with the very real threat of a meaningful decline in the rate of growth of corporate earnings.

Before we begin our discussion of the corporate profit bubble, however, it's necessary to define the ways in which this bubble is both similar to and different from the other bubbles that have already been examined. First of all, we believe certain elements of this bubble are more sustainable in the longer-term than the housing bubble and the global liquidity bubble. This is because the Law of Comparative Advantage has enabled corporate profits to remain permanently higher than in decades past. Without the Law of Comparative Advantage and without globalization, the corporate profit bubble would certainly burst, as the arbitrage between labor and capital among countries would no longer function with the same high levels of efficiency and profitability. But since globalization is, for the most part, an irreversible trend, corporate profits will continue to be at high levels relative to GDP by sheer virtue of the Law of Comparative Advantage. Therefore, the corporate profit bubble is less fragile than the other two bubbles under discussion, and, if it does burst, it will do so much more slowly.

Globalization, therefore, has led corporate profits to resilient record highs. But the other driver of the recent boom in corporate profits is the interest rate, and this is what gives us cause for concern. While globalization has resulted in relatively sustainable profit growth, we believe the low interest rate environment of the past several years has resulted in an element of *un*sustainable profit growth. If our argument is true, it is reasonable to assume that, as interest rates rise, corporate profit growth rates will be negatively affected. The Law of Comparative Advantage, however, should ensure that corporate profits will not decrease with quite the same speed or magnitude as housing prices or global liquidity.

To show why the corporate profit bubble should start to burst under the pressure of rising interest rates and other related factors, we would like to present an analytical framework developed by Doug Cliggott, CIO of Race Point Asset Management. Given the aforementioned resilience of the corporate profit bubble, this framework should give us a better understanding of how profit growth is created and, alternatively, how it can be destroyed. If we understand this phenomenon, we have a better chance of predicting when and how corporate profits could come under a serious potential threat from the global economy at large.

This framework starts with an equation for gross domestic product (GDP): the first equation most of us saw in Economics 101. Gross domestic product is the sum of four variables—consumption (C), investment spending (I), government spending (G), and the difference between exports (X) and imports (M). Therefore, GDP (represented as Y) is expressed by this equation:

$$Y = C + I + G + (X - M)$$

Now, let's revisit Figure 2.4, which shows that GDP and corporate profits (or earnings) have historically tracked each other with remarkable consistency. With the information provided in Figure 2.4, we can intuit that, if the variables in the above equation drive GDP growth, they could also drive corporate profit growth. Indeed, according to Cliggott and the *New York Times,* "there has been an 'almost perfect correlation' between corporate profits" and these four factors.[3]

With this assumption in place, we can use the drivers of GDP growth to create an equation for the growth of corporate profits. Bear with us here, as the algebra becomes longer, but it still is the Economics 101 concept of $C + I + G + (X - M) = GDP$.

The drivers of corporate profits over the near term can be defined as the sum of four variables:

$$C - DPI =$$

Where C is consumption and DPI is disposable personal income. When consumption exceeds disposable personal income, it is an additional driver for profits. As our net savings rate in the United States fell below zero over the past four years, this decrement became additive to profits. The opposite is true as well. When net savings become positive again, as it will when interest rates rise, profits will be negatively impacted.[4]

$$I = BI + RI$$

The variable I represents investment spending by businesses (structures and equipment) and residential investment. When business spending (BI) is increasing, as it is now, profits are helped. The same concept applies to residential investment spending (RI). Here, however, the bloom is off the rose and a decline in the level of residential spending is already well underway, as noted in the first section of this chapter.

$$G - T =$$

Government spending minus tax receipts. Government spending net of tax receipts (the fiscal deficit) has soared under the Bush administration and has significantly helped profits. This gap is narrowing and that process will hurt profit growth.

$$X - M =$$

Exports minus imports have risen substantially and represent a drag on profits. Should this change through a falling dollar, profits will benefit. Should the trade deficit worsen, the opposite is true.*

Now that we have defined these four variables, we are ready to present the next formula:

---

*There are instances in which certain components of the $(X - M)$ variable could have a different impact on the profit equation than the one outlined here. Specifically, it should be noted that many American corporations manufacture abroad, which means that a reduction in M may decrease their profits. That is, companies that make money through imports will suffer from the falling dollar.

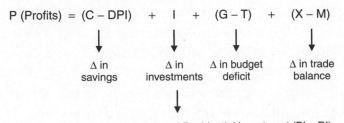

The purpose of this new formula is to provide an accurate way of predicting the future movements of corporate profits by using the variables that are usually characterized as driving GDP.* Because GDP growth and corporate profit growth have been shown to track each other over time, this model uses GDP-related inputs to estimate the parallel trends in corporate profits. If we can make reasonably correct assumptions about the upcoming changes to each of these variables, we can determine whether or not a bursting of the corporate profit bubble is truly in the cards.

The first step, however, is to see if this model actually works. The best way to validate the model's predictive powers is to see how well it can recapitulate the current corporate profit numbers. To do so, we turn to the *Flow of Funds Accounts of the United States,* a quarterly statistical review published by the Federal Reserve. For our purposes, we will use the numbers from the Q2-06 review, which was issued on September 19, 2006, to provide the inputs for our corporate profit equation.

Let's plug these numbers into the four variables in Cliggott's equation. The first variable is C – DPI or personal consumption expenditures minus disposable personal income. According to the Federal Reserve, personal consumption expenditures have risen from $7.065 trillion to $8.742 trillion

---

*This formula takes into account that aggregate year-to-year changes in depreciation and dividends are small and can be ignored for the present purpose.

from 2001 to 2005 for a net increase of $1.67 trillion. Mean-while, disposable personal income rose from $7.487 trillion to $9.036 trillion: an increase of $1.549 trillion. Subtracting $1.549 trillion from $1.687 trillion gives us $138 billion, the number by which spending exceeded income. In terms of our corporate profits equation, we refer to this difference as a profit accelerant. It is important to note that this profit accelerant cannot exist indefinitely. At some point, it is inevitable that savings will rise, and this will result in a drag on profit growth rates in upcoming quarters.

Next, let us turn to investment, the second variable in our equation. This variable is comprised of BI + RI, or business investment plus residential investment. Business investment, which consists of fixed investments in structures and equipment, rose from $1.177 trillion in 2001 to $1.266 trillion in 2005: a relatively minor change of $89 billion. Conversely, residential investment, which reflects housing expenditures, boomed over this period, rising from $469 billion to $770 billion for a change of $301 billion. Given our previous discussion of the housing bubble, this boom should come as no surprise. Like the C – DPI differential, the comparable excess portion of residential spending is a profit accelerant. However, with residential spending now in decline, the accelerant from housing has already become a negative for corporate profits going forward.

Let us now look at the third variable: G – T or government spending minus tax receipts, which represents the fiscal deficit in both the state and federal categories. In 2001, government spending on the state level was $1.368 trillion and rose to $1.704 trillion in 2005 for a gain of $336 billion. State tax receipts however, grew from $1.373 trillion to $1.704 trillion for a difference of $328 billion, approximately the same as the increase in state government spending. The state subcategory of this variable, therefore, exerted a neutral accelerant impact on corporate profits during the time period under analysis.

On the federal side, however, tax receipts rose $231 billion over the 2001 to 2005 period while expenditures soared by a net increase of $586 billion. If we subtract the increase in federal tax receipts from the increase in federal expenditures, it results in an increase to the fiscal deficit of $355 billion: a whopping accelerant to profits.

So far, we have seen that the first three drivers of GDP growth were decidedly positive for corporate profits over the 2001 to 2005 period. However, the fourth component in this framework, $X - M$, or exports minus imports, or net exports, was quite negative for profits. From the *Flow of Funds* report, we can determine that net exports in 2001 was a negative number: a deficit of $367 billion to be exact. Over the next four years, that number fell even further into negative territory, reaching a deficit of $717 billion in 2005. This resulted in a decrease to net exports of $350 billion, which reflected the fact that our nation's imports vastly exceed its exports. In terms of our equation, this represented a big drag on GDP and, by corollary, a detriment to reported profits.

Let us now put these numbers in one place. Each of these numbers represents the change in one of the four components of GDP. And because we know that change in corporate profits mirrors change in GDP, the total of these numbers should be reasonably close to the reported net gain in corporate profits from 2001 to 2005. Table 6.1 shows our results.

As reported in the *Flow of Funds* review, the actual change in reported profits for the period was $615 billion. The predictive power of our model, therefore, appears very strong.

Now that we've confirmed that our model works, let's use it to make some predictions about the future of corporate profits. Before we look into the future, however, it is important to remember that all four of these variables were turbocharged over the past four years by various accelerants within the marketplace—three positively and one negatively. We know that

TABLE 6.1   Inputs for Changes in Corporate Profits Equation, 2001–2005
($ in billions)

Personal consumption expenditures	
– Disposable personal income	$138
Business investment + Residential investment	
+ Change in private inventories	443
Government (Federal + State) spending	
– Government receipts	364
Exports – Imports	−350
	$595

the first three inputs—(C – DPI), (BI + RI), and (G – T)—were all positive contributors to profits over the 2001 to 2005 period. Consumption, fueled by low interest rates, grew faster than disposable personal income growth and this difference meaningfully added to corporate profit growth. The increase in investment spending was substantially due, in large part, to the above-trend growth rate in residential investment spending: again, the result of low interest rates. The fiscal deficit soared because government spending vastly exceeded tax receipts, and this scenario had a very positive effect on corporate profits. The one drag on profits was the increasing trade deficit, as imports grew at a faster pace than exports. However, this import/export imbalance was not big enough to slow down the boom in corporate profit growth during the 2001 to 2005 period.

Now, as we project these results into the future, we must take into consideration the fact that all of the variables that served as accelerants to profits, residential housing in particular, have put their glory days behind them. These three variables are all well past their respective points of inflection and, in our view, have begun to move in the opposite (i.e., negative) direction.

With (C – DPI), we believe that consumption will rise, but at a decreasing rate. Additionally, the consumer cannot continue to dis-save, especially with interest rates on the rise. So, the C – DPI gap must decline. If consumption falls below disposable personal income growth, C – DPI will turn negative, which means that savings will grow, and will therefore be a drag on corporate profit growth.

As for (BI + RI), residential investment will certainly decline from present levels simply because this component of total investment in relation to GDP is currently far above any U.S. historical average level. This variable will therefore exert a decidedly negative influence on continued growth in corporate profits.

As for (G – T), government spending will also rise, but the gap between spending and receipts will likely narrow, causing this variable to lose some of its momentum as a positive contributor to profits.

Our final variable, the trade deficit or (X – M), is the one potential bright spot in this prediction of future corporate profit levels, but it's ability to boost profits is contingent to some extent on the dollar falling. Should the dollar decline (as we believe it will) and should oil prices fall, the trade deficit should reverse itself in part. This scenario would benefit corporate profits.

Nevertheless, it seems no matter what scenario one might anticipate, corporate profits must slow, possibly to a very significant degree. Cliggott's work indicates an actual decline in profits in 2007, but our guess is that profit growth in 2007 will remain positive but fall into single digits, with the swing factor being changes in the trade deficit.

At this point, to clarify our overall argument, we should return to the GDP/profit graph (Figure 2.4) in order to explain the occasional divergences between these two data sets. From studying this graph, you have probably already noticed that there are times during which profit growth seems to fluctuate while GDP growth remains relatively consistent. Since, according to our model, changes in GDP and changes in corporate profits should run in parallel, wouldn't such a discrepancy appear to undermine the framework put forth in this chapter? The answer is that, while profits tend to mirror gains in nominal GDP growth over the long term, this is not always the case over the short term. In certain periods, unit labor costs and various other components of GDP can vary markedly from longer-term trends. In the current situation, it has been the combination of falling unit labor costs and the expanded use of debt by the consumer and the federal government that has driven much of the growth in corporate profits. In our view, these forces that aided rapid profit growth are about to disappear and, when they do, the rate of profit growth and the rate of GDP growth could diverge. This, however, should rectify itself in the long term and the value of our model should remain intact.

In summary, we've just determined that there are many drivers that contribute to the growth or decline of GDP and, by extension, the growth or decline of corporate profits. Interest rates, because they influence everything from consumer spending to residential investment to the import/export balance, will play a key role in determining to what extent the recent growth in corporate profits can continue. Based on the above analysis, we foresee a situation under which the corporate profit bubble could begin to deflate. If this deflation becomes severe enough to constitute a "burst," our marketplace could experience another instance of Punctuated Equilibrium.

Conclusion—Don't Ignore the Bursting Bubbles

We've just spent Chapter 6 attempting to outline the causes and consequences of three financial bubbles, each of which has been created or directly impacted by the recent movement in interest rates. Despite the abundance of evidence that points to the clear potential for a new instance of punctuated equilibrium, there are those who continue to believe that these changes will not take the form of a punctuation at all. Rather, these members of the investment community cling to the notion that these bursting bubbles will affect our marketplace in a manner that lacks the dramatic paradigm shifts that we anticipate. To refute this notion and to conclude this chapter, we look once again to the natural sciences.

More than 20 years ago, an article appeared in *Natural History Magazine* entitled "The History of Rainmaking." This article dealt with the influence of wishes and how they establish beliefs which in turn determine behavior.

This article asserted that, as man transitioned from the role of hunter to that of farmer, it dawned on him that if he could control the rain, the crops would not wither and die. The wish to control the rain led to a belief that it could be done.

Almost immediately, thousands of people came out of the woodwork claiming they could make it rain. Hence, the origin of the word "rainmaker." The belief in these rainmakers was faith-based, but empirically lacking. In other words, the rainmakers did sometimes seem to bring forth the rain, but this was never anything more than sheer coincidence. However, the wish for rain was strong enough that it made these random occurrences appear to justify the erroneous belief in the rainmakers' abilities.

According to the author of this article, this was another instance of a scenario that has since been replayed throughout the centuries and on every continent. As human beings, we have an astounding propensity to allow our wishes to determine our beliefs. And, with these beliefs established, the ground has been and always will be fertile for the rainmakers who choose to prey upon the believers.

Even in today's investment landscape, this age-old inter-
play of wishes, beliefs and behaviors is still at work. Specifically, a wish for the continuation of a robust and rapidly
growing equity market has led to several incorrect beliefs
about the market's impending slowdown. Those who choose
to let their wishes guide their beliefs ascribe to the "soft land-
ing" theory; they say that the bubbles may burst, but we will
barely notice the impact. Similarly, they believe that the bursting of these bubbles will occur in isolated, localized sectors,
and not in the national economy as a whole. These beliefs are
as foolish and ill-informed as thinking that a human being can
control the rain.

It is in this spirit that Chapter 6 was written: with the hope
that, when armed with the facts of our current investment landscape, the informed investor can realize the magnitude of these
bubbles and thus survive the punctuations to the equilibrium
that could occur when they burst. It is only by fully acknowl-
edging the realities of the marketplace that investors can protect and grow capital. The next and final chapter of this book
shows the reader how the application of the Shareholder Yield
philosophy can help to achieve precisely such goals.

PART THREE

Strategies for the New Investment Landscape

CHAPTER 7

Investing in Today's Capital Markets

We believe our primary function as professional investment managers is to be of use to the informed investor. Because of this, we realize the prior two parts of our book have only told part of the story. While we hope the preceding six chapters have been informative, thought-provoking, and engaging, they have done the potential disservice of dividing a unified investment philosophy into many seemingly disparate pieces. We have done this for the sake of clarity and completeness, but we understand that the informed investor seeks a more cohesive strategy. For this reason, we now provide a synthesis of the previous chapters.

This book has covered a considerable amount of territory, and although we have divided this territory into separate parts and chapters, we hope that the linkages in Figure 7.1 provide a good illustration of the fact that nothing in today's investment landscape can or should be dealt with in isolation. We encourage you to approach this final chapter with this dynamic and flexible investment philosophy in mind.

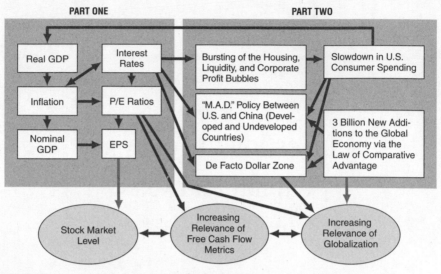

FIGURE 7.1   Interacting Forces within Today's Investment Landscape

The Case for Shareholder Yield

Before we discuss the specifics of our approach to stock selection and portfolio construction, let's attempt to better distill the message of the previous six chapters. What Figure 7.1 does in a diagram, the points below do in words:

1. The order of the three drivers of equity return is changing:
   a. Interest rates will stay flat or rise for the foreseeable future.
   b. Hence, P/E ratios (one of the drivers of equity returns) will stay flat or fall.
   c. To the extent that equities deliver positive returns, such positive returns will, out of necessity, be driven by dividends and earnings (the other two drivers of equity returns). Remember that, because the accepted lexicon of the investment world is still built around earnings-related concepts, we must use the terms "dividends" and "earnings" as a proxy for free cash flow-based metrics.

2. As the order of the drivers of equity return change in importance, preferred investment valuation metrics are also changing. Specifically, free cash flow metrics (as exemplified by their application in defining Shareholder Yield) will surpass traditional accounting metrics as the superior manner in which to evaluate investments:

   a. Through the use of *financial* metrics (free cash flow) rather than *accounting* metrics (e.g., P/E, P/BV) it is easier for the investor to discern those firms most likely to utilize their free cash flow intelligently for shareholder value creation.

   b. There are only five potential uses of free cash flow: (1) cash dividends, (2) share buybacks, (3) debt paydowns, (4) acquisitions, and (5) reinvestment in the business.

   c. The first three free cash flow deployment options define Shareholder Yield. The final two options generate firm growth.

   d. Conceptually, there is a simple way to figure out which category of free cash flow deployment a company should implement. If the return on incremental capital to be deployed for the two "firm growth" options (acquisitions or reinvestment) is not equal to or greater than the current average cost of capital, then capital should be returned to shareholders instead.

   e. Returning capital to shareholders is achieved by utilizing the cash flow deployment options that comprise Shareholder Yield: (1) cash dividends, (2) share buybacks, and (3) debt paydowns.

   f. By assembling a portfolio of companies that offer superior Shareholder Yield characteristics, an investor will be able to realize performance superior to that of the broad-based equity market in an environment in which P/E ratios are not likely to expand.

3. Several important themes within the present and future investment landscape have impacted and have been impacted by each aspect of the scenario listed previously:

    a. Globalization continues to allocate labor and capital via the Law of Comparative Advantage. This process has kept inflation down, kept interest rates relatively low, and has resulted in remarkable increases in productivity and profits. As globalization continues to impact our international economy, a free cash flow-oriented investment philosophy will be more important than ever.

    b. The continuation of interest rates at present levels may well result in the popping of three big economic bubbles: (1) the housing bubble, (2) the global liquidity bubble, and (3) the corporate profit bubble. Because interest rates are also extremely integral to the notion of Shareholder Yield, the popping of these bubbles cannot help but influence how both companies and investors use free cash flow as the dominant investment metric.

Using Shareholder Yield to Protect and Grow Invested Capital

This book's final task is to express the manner in which the Shareholder Yield philosophy can be incorporated into the processes of stock selection and portfolio construction. At Epoch Investment Partners, we have built two mutual funds that are managed through a Shareholder Yield-derived methodology.* To demonstrate how Shareholder Yield can be employed as a mean-

---

*In the United States, this fund is the Epoch Global Equity Shareholder Yield Fund (Bloomberg symbol: EPSYX, web site: http://theworldfunds.com). In Canada, this fund is the CI Funds Global Dividends Advantage Fund (web site: www.cifunds.com).

ingful investment tool, we will discuss the ways in which we have designed these funds to both protect and grow invested capital.

There are four core requirements for the creation of a Shareholder Yield-focused portfolio. The first requirement is the realization of an exceptional, robust current cash dividend yield. (Think approximately 4.5 percent.) Ideally, this yield should compare favorably to that of the long bond and should be much greater than that of the global equity indices. (Think 200 basis points or more.) Second, we seek to build a portfolio that will provide a consistency of dividend growth; we benchmark to a trailing 3-year compound annual dividend growth rate of 3 percent. Third, we design the portfolio to display global participation and diversification, not only across countries and regions but also across sectors. The fourth requirement is that the portfolio is balanced in such a way as to reduce risk and to provide a minimum of variance around a portfolio's mean expected return. That is, we ensure that no one security is responsible for an overly significant portion of the portfolio's total yield. This is one of the ways in which our approach differs from many of the other funds that offer a dividend-specific product. Other funds often assign a stronger weighting within the portfolio to the stocks that produce the highest dividend yields. At Epoch Investment Partners, however, we prefer to maintain a more evenly-weighted equilibrium among securities. In this way, we reduce the risks associated with the performance or income variability of any particular stock.

With these four requirements in mind, we then identify the potential universe of companies that are utilizing their free cash flow according to the principles of Shareholder Yield: that is, deploying cash flow via cash dividends, share repurchases and debt paydown. Given that we seek to build global portfolios, this universe begins with a list of over 10,000 names; this list is comprised of the securities in the S&P/Citigroup BMI World Index and all ADRs listed on U.S. exchanges. To narrow down this universe, our first step is the application of a proprietary quantitative screen which seeks to identify a subgroup of stocks with several specific characteristics. First of all, this screen is built to recognize stocks that display high (4 percent or higher) current dividend incomes relative to peers and alternatives. Second, we seek stocks that show positive operating cash flow growth over the past five years. Specifically, we want to find companies that have increased dividends in more than 50 percent of the years in their available historical data. Along these lines, it is important that the most recent dividend history possess three or more years of monotonically increasing dividends; that is, dividends should increase in a step-wise manner with each successive year. The third criterion within this proprietary screening process is the identification of companies whose cash from operations exceeds dividends over a trailing 3-year period. This requirement is necessary to ensure that the stocks in our portfolios possess ample dividend coverage. Finally, we want to find companies for whom the dividend is "sacred." This means we seek companies that have not cancelled their dividends at any point within their available financial history (20-years maximum).

After the implementation of our screening process, we arrive at a group of approximately 200 candidate stocks. Of these 200, approximately 50 percent survive further individual analysis and are included in the portfolio. An additional set of stocks are included that are not subject to the screen but are incorporated into our candidate universe because we believe they will pursue a Shareholder Yield-based cash deployment strategy in the future. From here, we subject each of these stock to rigorous, free cash flow-focused fundamental analysis before earmarking them for eventual inclusion into the portfolio. This is the point at which our evaluation process acquires a layer of qualitative decision making in the vein of traditional equity research.

As the portfolio is assembled, we select stocks in the hope of meeting the following goals. First of all, we endeavor to realize a high conventional dividend yield well in excess of 4 percent, and recent dividend growth in excess of 3 percent per annum. Therefore, the expected minimum incremental yield per year is anticipated to be approximately 13 to 15 basis points. In addition, the portfolio is designed such that the influence of special dividends will not positively skew the realized yield. Finally, we expect the portfolio to generate an additional 1.5 percent yield through share repurchases and debt reductions, thus incorporating each of the three components of the Shareholder Yield philosophy. As you might expect in the current environment of highly liquid public corporate balance sheets, share repurchases within the portfolio exceed debt reductions by a large margin.

The final element of the portfolio construction process is the implementation of position constraints designed to limit the impact of any one security to the success of the portfolio as a whole. In this way, we minimize the risk surrounding the portfolio's expected return. The first position constraint dictates that the minimum position in a stock should be equal to 0.50 percent of the portfolio, with a maximum position of 2.5 percent. We also limit the maximum dividend income contribution per security to 3 percent of the portfolio's total dividend income. This ensures that, should a company in the portfolio eliminate its dividend, the negative effect to the portfolio's cash dividend yield would not exceed 3 percent of the expected portfolio yield; or roughly 15 basis points. Similarly, the maximum contribution of a security to the expected incremental income growth of the portfolio is 5 percent.

With the stock selection and portfolio construction processes completed in the manner described above, the investor should be able to realize a total return that will likely exceed average equity market returns on a long-term, absolute basis, given that P/E ratios are likely to be neutral at best going forward. Similarly, the portfolio will be highly diversified in order to ensure optimal risk management.

In summary,* we believe the Shareholder Yield philosophy can be a foundation for successful stock selection and portfolio construction strategies. In employing these strategies, we seek to create funds that deliver returns of 8 to 10 percent with the least possible volatility surrounding that objective, and that will capture the opportunities inherent in the ongoing globalization of today's investment landscape.

Conclusion

To end this book, we'd like to leave you with the most important conclusions that can be derived from the past several chapters. First of all, there are two concepts that stand out as the drivers behind our investment strategy and the behavior of the equity markets as a whole:

1. *Interest rates:* With the decline in interest rates over the 1980 to 2000 period, the table was set for the rise of Shareholder Yield as a dominant component of total equity returns. Now, as interest rates are likely to stay flat or rise, pricing multipliers (P/Es) are out and real economic drivers (dividends and earnings/cash flow) are in. In addition, the decline and subsequent increase in interest rates provides the stimulus for the upcoming "punctuations" to our market equilibrium.
2. *Globalization:* Globalization is the unprecedented phenomenon that is currently magnifying, connecting, and accelerating everything that happens within the investment landscape.

An informed investment strategy in today's market either originates from or can be traced back to these two interrelated concepts.

---

*For the first ten months of 2006, the U.S. fund (EPSYX) gained 19.1% net of all expenses.

In the process of deciding on our parting words of advice, an oft-repeated truism has consistently come to mind: the more things change, the more things stay the same. When I was a boy mowing lawns and trimming hedges, I was focused on one thing: generating cash flow and using it in the best possible way. Back then, I never would have thought that, upon growing up to become a seasoned investment manager, my priorities would remain exactly the same. But, to my surprise, my experience on Wall Street has only reinforced the principles of free cash flow deployment that I first learned decades ago. Whether mowing lawns in the 1950s or making informed investments in the new millennium, one thing is certain. It's all about free cash flow, and it always will be, no matter how much the investment landscape changes around us.

Finally, we'd like to leave you with the two images that, in our mind, encapsulate the argument for a free cash flow-oriented investment strategy that incorporates the concept of Shareholder Yield (Figures 7.2 and 7.3).

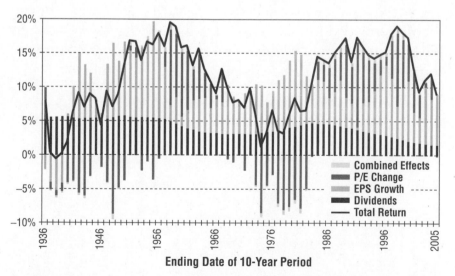

FIGURE 7.2   Components of Compound Annual Total Returns for Trailing 10-Year Periods (S&P 500 Composite 1936–2005).

Source: Standard & Poor's.

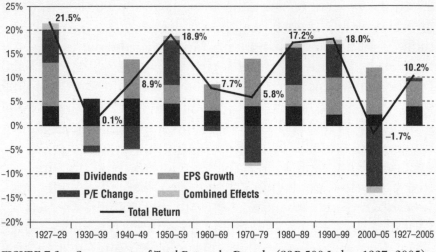

FIGURE 7.3   Components of Total Return by Decade (S&P 500 Index, 1927–2005).
Source: Standard & Poor's.

To use another popular truism, we believe that a compelling picture speaks much louder than words. In writing this book, we have endeavored only to clarify and empower the picture provided in these two images. In doing so, we hope to have offered the global investor a new set of priorities for how to profit from the changing sources of equity returns.

Continuous-Time Free Cash Flow Valuation Framework

The appendix presents a cash flow forecasting model that is currently under development at Epoch Investment Partners.* The following analysis will provide some quantitative details about our security selection process.

Free Cash Flow Valuation and the Epoch Core Model

The purpose of security analysis for investing in a firm is to research the risk and return characteristics of the underlying *business process* employed by the firm to generate profit. Following the Modigliani-Miller Theory and Merton's structural model, a firm is treated as an interest rate derivative whose payoff is contingent upon its underlying business risk; its capital structure is designed to maximize the shareholder value; its *enterprise valuation* can be determined by a replicating strategy based on no-arbitrage assumption. For firms competing in

---

*We are grateful to the Epoch Investment Partners quantitative research team for providing this analysis, particularly Thomas Yitien Hu.

the same business environment, the true valuation metrics that differentiate them are the firm's *distribution policy* and *investment strategy* with respect to its cash flow. We recognize there are only five options[1] a firm can explore with its excess cash in order to maximize shareholder value:

1. Pay cash dividends;
2. Repurchase outstanding shares;
3. Reduce outstanding debts;
4. Engage in mergers & acquisitions;
5. Reinvest in internal projects with favorable returns.

By this construction, *free cash flow,* or the cash available for distribution to investors after all planned capital investment and taxes, is the key driver in assessing the value of a firm.

To wit, *a free cash flow discount model* postulates that the firm value V can be derived by discounting a perpetual free cash flow generated by the firm as follows:

$$V = S + D = \hat{\mathbb{E}}\left(\frac{\widetilde{FCP}}{\rho\left(\bar{f}\left(t, T\right), R_M\right)} \right)$$

where S and D represent the value of the firm's equity and debt, and $\hat{\mathbb{E}}$ denotes a *valuation measure* adjusted by the firm's *weighted average cost of capital* (WACC), ρ, given by

$$\rho = k_E \frac{S}{S + D} + k_D \left(1 - \tau\right) \frac{D}{S + D}$$

where τ is the effective tax rate and k_E and k_D denote the firm's cost of equity and cost of debt, whose value can be estimated from market-observable parameters $\bar{f}\left(t,\ T\right)$ and R_M, the risky corporate yield curve and the benchmark return via multifactor[2] Capital Asset Pricing Model (CAPM).

If these parameters can be reliably extracted from liquid market data, then security analysis is essentially forecasting the firm's future free cash flow and contemplating the viability of the firm's capital structure. Principal investment and trading decisions can thus be made according to such a forecast. An investor can express his or her views on the firm's business outlook by positioning in an appropriate tranche in the firm's capital structure via trading related financial instruments.

It has been a well-known fact that forecasting free cash flow using publicly available information is hard due to the difficulty in distinguishing capital expenditure for business expansion and essential maintenance. For firms going through special situations such as leveraged recapitalization, leveraged buyouts, spin-offs, carve-outs, financial distress, and IPOs, or experiencing regime shift in the competitive environment, the free cash flow implied by the financial statements and pricing information observed in the markets must be used with caution.

Recognizing that security analysis is more of an art than science, we have developed the *Epoch Core Model:* an evolving proprietary research platform that blends the fundamental insights and quantitative rigor for forecasting free cash flow.

In the Epoch Core Model, the forecasting procedure is built into the selection algorithm that seeks to identify firms that are forward cash-rich and exhibit financial flexibility in exploring strategic real options. A firm's common stock will be issued a favorable rank by the Core Model if it shows:[3]

- High median forecast of earnings per share for the next twelve months;
- High dividend yield for the last twelve months;
- Stable trend in capital expenditure for the last twelve quarters;

■ Low debt-to-equity ratio;

■ Low dividend payout ratio.

This procedure, though qualitatively feasible, produces no measurable quantity related to the firm's free cash flow. To enhance this procedure, we propose a *forward* free cash flow model based on forecasting a firm's *revenues*. By starting from the top line, we believe this methodology provides a scalable framework for analysts to issue recommendations based on forecast of the firm's business risk and its free cash flow implications given the firm's incumbent capital structure.

Free Cash Flow Forecasting Model: A Continuous-Time Approach

We define a firm's free cash flow as follows:[4]

R_t :   firm's revenues at time t;

$c_0 + c_1 R_t$:   firm's operating overheads, assumed linearly dependent on revenues;

τ :   effective tax rate;

DA :   depreciation and amortization;

ΔNWC :   increase (decrease) in net working capital;

$CapEx$:   capital expenditure;

$$\widetilde{FCF_t} = (1-\tau)\big(\underbrace{R_t - c_0 - c_1 R_t}_{EBIT}\big) + DA - \Delta NWC - CapEx$$

$$= (1-\tau)(1-c_1)R_t - (1-\tau)c_0 + DA - \Delta NWC - CapEx$$

$$= \alpha + \beta R_t$$

We assume that the fixed portion of the firm's operating overhead c_0 and other accrual items can be approximated by a constant a for analytical tractability.

By decomposing a firm's free cash flow in this form, we have separated its risk exposure into a systemic component, βR_t, and an idiosyncratic component, α. The firm's enterprise value under free cash flow discount model given its WACC then becomes

$$V_t = \frac{\alpha}{(1-\tau)k_D} + \frac{\beta R_t}{\rho - g}$$

where g is the growth rate of revenues. We discount the fixed component of free cash flow at the after-tax cost of debt because this component is assumed to have no exposure to market risk and can be collateralized to service the firm's debt issuance.

To determine R_t, the revenue process of a firm, we assume it obeys geometric Brownian motion with constant[5] drift g and constant volatility σ under suitable probability measure:

$$R_t = R_0 + \int_0^t gR_s\,ds + \int_0^t \sigma R_s\,d\hat{W}_s$$

or in stochastic differential equation form:

$$\frac{dR_t}{R_t} = g\,dt + \sigma\,d\hat{W}_t$$

whose solution is given by

$$R_t = R_0 \exp\left\{\left(g - \frac{1}{2}\sigma^2\right)t + \sigma\hat{W}_t\right\}$$

thanks to Itô's lemma. Since the Wiener process $\hat{W}_t$ is normally distributed with mean 0 and variance t, we can estimate g and σ by using Mean $\left(\ln \dfrac{R_t}{R_{t-dt}} \right) = g\,dt$ and Var $\left(\ln \dfrac{R_t}{R_{t-dt}} \right) = \sigma^2 dt$.

Thus we can derive a discretized model of R_t in the following form:

$$\Delta R_t = R_{t+\Delta t} - R_t = gR_t \Delta t + \sigma R_t \sqrt{\Delta t}\, \epsilon_t$$

where ϵ_t denotes a series of independent and identically distributed normal random variables. We thus have the Δt-ahead predictor of the revenue process at $t + \Delta t$ conditional on the observed revenue at time t:

$$R_{t+\Delta t} = (1 + g\Delta t)R_t + \sigma R_t \sqrt{\Delta t}\, \epsilon_t$$

where Δt is the natural reporting frequency of the firm's financials in terms of year fraction, i.e., $\Delta t = \frac{1}{4}$ for quarterly and $\frac{1}{12}$ for monthly revenue series.

The Δt-ahead predictor of the firm's free cash flow process is therefore

$$\begin{aligned}\widetilde{FCF}_{t+\Delta t} &= \alpha + \beta R_{t+\Delta t} \\ &= \alpha + \beta(1 + g\Delta t)R_t + \beta\sigma R_t \sqrt{\Delta t}\, \epsilon_t\end{aligned}$$

and its expected forward enterprise value under the WACC-adjusted probability measure:

$$\hat{V}_{t+\Delta t} = \hat{\mathbb{E}}\left(\widetilde{\frac{FCF_{t+\Delta t}}{\rho}}\right)$$

$$= \alpha\int_{0}^{\infty} e^{-(1-\tau)\,k_{D}t}\,dt + \beta\int_{0}^{\infty} e^{-\rho t}\hat{\mathbb{E}}\left(R_{t+\Delta t}\right)dt$$

$$= \frac{\alpha}{\left(1-\tau\right)k_{D}} + \frac{\beta\hat{R}_{t+\Delta t}}{\rho - g}$$

The next key step is to find the appropriate discount rate given the firm's business risk. We briefly outline the methodology to estimate these parameters from market information in the following sections.

Construct Default-Free Discount Curve

We bootstrapp the discount factors from market prices of instruments traded in the inter-bank markets: (i) cash instruments in money markets (1 day to 9 months); (ii) interest rate futures (e.g., Eurodollar futures) contracts (6 months to 2 years); (iii) interest rate swap contracts (1 year to 30 years). Cash securities are quoted on a simple spot rate basis $f(0, t)$. The quoted price simply indicates the annualized simple interest rate the borrower will pay to the lender according to Act/360 day-count convention. The discount factor is given by

$$D\left(0, t\right) = \frac{1}{1 + f\left(0, t\right)\times\dfrac{t}{360}}$$

where t is the tenor of the securities.

Eurodollar futures contracts are quoted on a simple forward rate basis $f(0, T, T+\delta)$ and settle according to the International Monetary Markets dates, i.e., the 3rd Wednesday of March, June, September, and December. The lender (futures buyer) can agree to place funds with the borrower (futures seller) during a future period $[T, T+\delta]$ (e.g., for three months between June 21, 2006 and September 20, 2006 for EDM6 Eurodollar futures contract) at a certain annualized simple interest rate $f(T, T+\delta)$. The price quoted needs to be adjusted for forward rate convexity. The calculation formula is given by

$$f\left(T, T+\delta\right) = 10,000 - P_{quoted} - \frac{Convexity}{10,000}$$

The discount factor implied is therefore (Act/360 daycount)

$$D\left(0, T+\delta\right) = \frac{D\left(0, T\right)}{1 + f\left(T, T+\delta\right) \times \dfrac{\delta}{360}}$$

Interest rate swap contracts are quoted in swap rates, which is the fixed rate the Payer (Receiver) needs to pay (receive) in a swap transaction to receive floating rate payment (e.g., 3-month LIBOR quarterly money) from the Receiver(Payer) on a notional amount till contract maturity. At trade inception the swap rate is so determined such that the transaction has net present value of zero. It can be shown that the swap rate of a liquid vanilla swap can be determined by the following relationship:

$$s\left(t, T_0, T_n\right) = \frac{D\left(t, T_0\right) - D\left(t, T_n\right)}{\sum_{i=1}^{n} \delta_n D\left(t, T_i\right)}$$

where t is the valuation date of a swap starting at T_0 and terminates at T_n with payment date $T_1, T_2, \ldots, T_{n-1}$ and $\delta_n := T_i - T_{i-1}$ is the tenor between payment dates according to given day-count convention.

Modeling Default Probabilities and Corporate Credit Spread

To estimate a firm's credit risk, we place ourselves on a filtered probability space $\left(\Omega, F, (F_t), \widetilde{\mathbb{P}}\right)$ and a fixed time horizon T^*.

Consider the *hazard rate* $\{h(t, \omega)\}t \leq T^*$ as a non-negative, continuous, adapted stochastic process. The *default time* is defined as a random stopping time

$$\tau(\omega) \triangleq \inf\left\{t \in \left[0, T^*\right] : \int_0^t h(s, \omega)\,ds \geq \theta\right\}$$

where θ is an exponential random variable with rate 1, independent of the hazard rate process. The *survival probability* $S(t)$ until time t is given by

$$S(t) \triangleq \widetilde{\mathbb{P}}\ (\tau > t) = \widetilde{\mathbb{E}}\left[\mathbb{1}_{\{\tau > t\}}\right]$$

If we assume $h(t)$ to be piecewise constant (or constant if we are courageous), then the survival probability simplifies to

$$S(t) = \exp\left(-\int_0^t h(u)\,du\right)$$

and the default arrival becomes an inhomogenous Poisson process. If h is constant, then the survival time follows an exponential distribution with parameter h and the default arrival is homogenous Poisson. These assumptions will not normally hold in practice but can serve as a reasonable approximation for analytical tractability.

Under this model we can estimate a firm's credit spread from its credit default swap (CDS) contracts. CDS is a bilateral contract that enables an investor to buy protection against the risk of default of an asset issued by a specified reference entity. The Protection Buyer pays a running premium (CDS spread) and receives contingent payment (loss given default, LGD) when a certain *credit event*[6] occurs, and must deliver the defaulted deliverable obligation referenced by the CDS to the protection Seller, who in principle can sell the defaulted obligation at recovery value. Let $t_1, t_2, \ldots, t_M$ be the payment dates for the premium leg. The protection buyer must pay this cash flow until default occurs, therefore the present value of the premium leg is

$$PL(t) = N \sum_{t_m \geq t} s_{cds} \delta_m \widetilde{\mathbb{E}} \left[D(t,\, t_m)\, \mathbb{1}_{\{\tau > t_m\}} \right]$$

where $T = t_M$ is the CDS maturity, $\delta_m := (t_m - t_{m-1})$ the tenor between payments, N the notional amount and $D(t,\, t_m)$ the discount factor between $[t,\, t_m]$. The present value of the default leg is

$$DL(t) = N\widetilde{\mathbb{E}} \left[\underbrace{\left(1 - R(\zeta,\, \tau)\right)}_{LGD} D(t,\, \tau) 1_{\{\tau \leq T\}} \right]$$

where $R(\zeta,\, \tau)$ is the recovery value, which may be dependent on default time τ and other economic or legal factor ζ. In practice we often assume R to be constant.

The fair CDS spread is found by equating the two legs such that the transaction has net present value of zero at inception:

$$s_{cds} = \frac{\widetilde{\mathbb{E}} \left[(1 - R) D(t,\, \tau)\, \mathbb{1}_{\{\tau \leq T\}} \right]}{\sum_{t_m \geq t} \delta_m \widetilde{\mathbb{E}} \left[D(t,\, t_m)\, \mathbb{1}_{\{\tau > t_m\}} \right]}$$

In practice we are given the information in the form of a CDS curve so that we may evaluate the mark-to-market value of a CDS via *bootstrapping procedure*[7] in order to back out the implied survival probabilities at each payment date. Because of its increasing popularity and liquidity, CDS has become accepted as the lead indicator of a firm's credit outlook. This approach allows us to build the implied hazard rate as well as a firm's credit curve $\bar{f}(t, T)$ that can be used as proxy to infer its cost of debt. We then combine this estimate with the firm's cost of equity based on CAPM to derive its weighted average cost of capital for valuation.

Implementation

We construct a simple screening algorithm in our proprietary research system to implement this forecast procedure as follows:

- Esitmate g and σ using reported quarterly LTM revenues over rolling five-year horizon;
- Derive current free cash flow and estimate α and β using the most recent LTM revenues;
- Compute 1Q-ahead predictor of free cash flow using the estimated parameters.

To evaluate the effectiveness of this forecast procedure, we calculate the forward *free cash flow yield,* i.e., $\dfrac{FCF_{t+\Delta t}}{\text{Market Value}_t}$ as well as the spot free cash flow yield for firms in our coverage universe and perform backtesting over the ranked universe[8] to see if it has any predictive power for the subsequent stock returns. We report the information coefficient[9] and t-statistics over various return horizons as follows:

FCF Yield IC/T-Stat	Spot	Forward
1M	0.05/3.02	0.05/3.00
3M	0.08/4.67	0.08/4.60
6M	0.11/6.11	0.11/5.97
12M	0.14/7.37	0.13/7.13

We can see the spot and the forward FCF yield have very similar predictive power; all are statistically significant at 5 percent level. This is not surprising because the forward free cash flow is inferred from the spot free cash flow and the most recently reported revenue. Since the forecast horizon is one quarter, the FCF process is unlikely to diffuse too far from its spot level. The correlation between the spot FCF yield and the forward FCF yield is 0.96 over the backtesting time frame, corroborating the above empirical observation.

Future Work

The need for improvement is obvious. By modeling the firm's revenues as a lognormal process, we are ignoring the nonstationary effect inherent in the economic environment. A robust FCF forecast model must take into consideration the sensitivities of the firm's business process to the macroeconomic parameters. Also, the linear relationship between revenues and free cash flow will break down[10] during corporate restructuring and regime shift in the competitive environment. To capture those effects we may construct a multivariate model based on balance sheet items. Potential problems exist due to the difficulty in specifying coherent distributions for those items and over-fitting might be hard to avoid. For this we must rely on experienced human judgment to identify catalysts likely to drive stock price movement. Finally, to further check its viability as in any derivatives pricing problem, the model should be able to calibrate to the firm's enterprise value observable in the market, given the cost of debt (estimated from its liquid debt securities or CDS curve) and the cost of equity (estimated under CAPM assumptions using proper equity benchmark). We defer the calibration and model enhancement steps to future research.

The free cash flow valuation framework presented here, though idealistic, provides the foundation for evaluating the firm's fair value consistent with the theory of modern corporate finance. By adopting a parsimonious approach, our estimation methodology allows qualitative judgment to be incorporated into quantitative framework in a robust manner. Furthermore, when evaluating the firm's entry/exit options, as well as other scenarios under special situations, this model can be more powerful than the traditional earnings-based methodology.

Chapter 1: Free Cash Flow

1. John Burr Williams, *The Theory of Investment Value* (Cambridge, MA: Harvard University Press, 1938) 55.

2. Enrique R. Arzac, *Valuation for Mergers, Buyouts, and Restructuring* (Hoboken, NJ: John Wiley & Sons, 2005) 9.

3. George C. Christy, *Free Cash Flow: A Two-Hour Primer for Management and the Board* (Booklocker.com, 2006) 6.

4. See note 3, p. 5.

5. See note 3, p. 10.

6. Jack Treynor, "Feathered Feast: A Case," *Financial Analysts Journal* (November/December 1993).

7. Source: Thomson Financial.

8. See note 3.

Chapter 2: The Sources of Equity Return

1. Merton H. Miller and Franco Modigliani, "The Cost of Capital, Corporation Finance and the Theory of Investment," *American Economic Review* (1958).

2. Source: Insurance Information Institute's "Financial Services Factbook."

3. "Unnatural Causes of Debt," *Economist,* September 16, 2006.

4. See note 3.

Chapter 3: Shareholder Yield in Depth

1. Ian McDonald, "Capital Pains: Big Cash Hoards," *Wall Street Journal,* July 21, 2006.
2. Gregory Peters, "US Credit Strategy—Two Words: Buybacks," *Morgan Stanley Research,* August 2, 2006.
3. Bruce Bartlett "Benefits of the Bush Dividend Tax Cut," *National Center for Policy Analysis,* August 27, 2004.
4. Jobs and Growth Tax Relief Reconciliation Act, ASA Dividend Scorecard, June 4, 2004.
5. Barry B. Burr, "Out of the Wilderness," *Pensions & Investments Online,* September 4, 2006.
6. Ian McDonald, "New Cash Cows: Biggest Stocks," *Wall Street Journal,* Friday, January 6, 2006.
7. *Barron's,* August 21, 2006.
8. Robert D. Arnott and Clifford S. Asness, "Surprise! Higher Dividends = Higher Earnings Growth," *Financial Analysts Journal,* January/February 2003.
9. See note 8.
10. See note 8.
11. Shirley A. Lazo, "Dividend Savant?" *Barron's,* August 21, 2006.
12. See note 11.
13. Henry McVey and David R. McNellis, "US Strategy—Secret Sauce II: Buybacks," *Morgan Stanley Equity Research,* July 19, 2006.
14. Bernard Condon, "Buyback Boomlet," *Forbes,* May 22, 2006.
15. Gregory Peters, "US Credit Strategy—Two Words: Buybacks," *Morgan Stanley Research,* August 2, 2006.
16. Source: TrimTabs Investment Research.
17. Citigroup Portfolio Strategist, January 5, 2006.
18. Henry H. McVey and David R. McNellis, "US Strategy—Secret Sauce II: Buybacks," *Morgan Stanley Equity Research,* July 19, 2006.
19. Citigroup Portfolio Strategist, January 5, 2006.
20. Floyd Norris, "In 2005, Companies Set a Record for Sharing with Shareholders," *New York Times,* January 7, 2006.

21. See note 20.
22. Andrew Bary, "Time to Buy," *Barron's,* July 24, 2006.
23. Fara Lupiano of CreditSights, *Barron's,* August 21, 2006.
24. Gregory Peters, "US Credit Strategy—Two Words: Buybacks," *Morgan Stanley Research,* August 2, 2006.
25. Amy Feldman, "Sending Out a Message by Buying Back Shares," *New York Times,* October 2, 2005.
26. Richard A. Brealey and Steward C. Myers, *Principles of Corporate Finance* (New York: McGraw-Hill, 1984) 357–358.
27. David Wyss, "Spend It as Fast as I Can: U.S. Economic Forecast Monthly Summary," *Standard & Poor's,* April 2006.
28. G. Bennett Stewart, *The Quest for Value* (New York: Harper-Collins, 1991).
29. Marc Hogan, "Heavy Debt, Big Worries?" *BusinessWeek.com,* August 2, 2006.

Chapter 4: Focus on Dividends

1. "In the Shadows of Debt," *Economist,* September 23, 2006.

Chapter 5: Globalization

1. International Monetary Fund, World Economic Outlook Database, September 2006.
2. Thomas L. Friedman, *The World Is Flat: A Brief History of the 21st Century* (New York: Farrar, Straus and Giroux, 2005) 226.
3. David J. Lynch, "Thanks to Its CEO, UPS Doesn't Just Deliver," *USA Today,* July 24, 2006.
4. "The New Titans," *Economist,* September 16, 2006.
5. "Unnatural Causes of Debt," *Economist,* September 16, 2006.
6. "The New Titans," *Economist,* September 16, 2006.
7. See note 6.
8. Clyde Prestowitz, *Three Billion New Capitalists: The Great Shifts of Wealth and Power to the East* (New York: Basic Books, 2005).
9. See note 6.

10. "China's Oil Consumption: Today's Editorial," *Washington Times,* April 20, 2006.

11. Source: British Petroleum.

12. "A Topsy-Turvy World," *Economist,* September 16, 2006.

13. Source: International Monetary Fund.

14. Nicholas R. Lardy, *Integrating China into the Global Economy* (Washington, DC: Brookings Institution Press, 2002) 80.

15. Clyde Prestowitz, *Three Billion New Capitalists: The Great Shifts of Wealth and Power to the East* (New York: Basic Books, 2005) 255.

Chapter 6: Interest Rates, Bubbles, and Punctuated Equilibriums

1. "Unluncky Ben Bernanke," *Grant's Interest Rate Observer,* October 6, 2002, p. 4.

2. Source: U.S. Census Bureau, August 2006.

3. Norm Alster, "Is the Corporate Profit Machine about to Sputter?" *New York Times,* October 1, 2006.

4. Martin Feldstein, "The Return of Savings," *Foreign Affairs,* May/June 2006.

Appendix: Continuous-Time Free Cash Flow Valuation Framework

1. We define the first three choices as *Shareholder Yield.*

2. We use benchmark equity risk premium and size premium as our primary and secondary factors.

3. This procedure is based on conversations with Joe Sroka, an insightful Epoch Analyst.

4. The following discussion follows Chapter 8 in *Valutation for Mergers, Buyouts, and Restructuring* by Enrique R. Arzac, Professor of Finance and Economics at the Columbia University Graduate School of Business.

5. Empirically, both g and σ are random and exhibit time-dependent and mean-reverting behavior. Lognormal assumption is but a mathematical convenience, as adopted in the classical Black-Scholes framework.

6. See 2003 ISDA Credit Derivatives Definitions for more details.

7. In reality we must use the discrete version of this model. Let $Q(0, t_m)$ be the survival probability up to time t_m ($\bar{Q}(0, 0) := 1$). If we assume defaults can only occur at *accrual dates,* then the premium leg and default leg can be rewritten as

$$PL(0) = N \sum_{m=1}^{M} s_{cds} \delta_m D(0, t_m) \bar{Q}(0, t_m);$$

$$DL(0) = N \sum_{m=1}^{M} (1-R) D(0, t_m) \left(\bar{Q}(0, t_{m-1}) - \bar{Q}(0, t_m) \right)$$

By equating the two legs we have a system of linear equations that can be solved recursively in most solver packages (e.g., Excel) to get $\bar{Q}(0, t_1)$, $\bar{Q}(0, t_2)$, ..., $\bar{Q}(0, t_M)$. However if the defaults can occur between accrual dates, define $\bar{Q}(t_m)$ $\triangleq \bar{Q}(0, t_m) - \bar{Q}(0, t_m-1)$ as the default probability during tenor δ_m and we can back out $\bar{Q}(0, t_m)$, $m = 1, \ldots M$ by solving

$$0 = \sum_{m=1}^{M} s_{cds} \left(\delta_m D(0, t_m) \bar{Q}(0, t_m) + \int_{t_{m-1}}^{t_m} (u - t_{m-1}) D(0, u) Q(du) \right)$$
$$- (1-R) \int_0^T D(0, u) Q(du)$$

and interpolate the survival probabilities between two accrual dates.

8. We rank the coverage universe by free cash flow yield into quintiles. Each quintile represents an equal-weighted portfolio. We backtest 15 years of data with monthly rebalancing.

9. This is the *Spearman*'s ρ, or rank correlation of the trading signal X and the subsequent returns Y. More specifically, let X_i, Y_i, $i = 1 \ldots n$ be the sample returns and signal series and n be the number of observations, then the sample Spearman's ρ is estimated by $1 - 6 \dfrac{\sum_{i=1}^{n} \left(\text{Rank}(X_i) - \text{Rank}(Y_i) \right)^2}{n(n^2 - 1)}$. Information coefficient can be related to the alpha of a strategy via the *Fundamental Law of Active Management:* $IR = IC \times \sqrt{BR}$, where *IR* is the manager's *information ratio* and *BR* is the strategy's *breadth,* or number of independent forecasts. For details, see Grinold and Kahn (1999).

10. We may alternatively define Free Cash Flow $\triangleq$ Net Operating Cash Flow—CapEx to account for this pitfall.

REFERENCES

Arzac, E. R. 2004. *Valuations for Mergers, Buyouts, and Restructuring.* Hoboken, NJ: John Wiley & Sons.

Duffie, D., and K. Singleton. 1999. "Modeling Term Structures of Defaultable Bonds." *Review of Financial Studies* 12, 687–720.

Grinold, R. C., and R. N. Kahn. 1999. *Active Portfolio Management: A Quantitative Approach for Producing Superior Returns and Controlling Risk.* New York: McGraw-Hill.

Ho, T., and S. Lee. 2004. *The Oxford Guide to Financial Modeling: Applications for Capital Markets, Corporate Finance, Risk Management and Financial Institutions.* New York: Oxford University Press.

Merton, R. C. 1974. On the Pricing of Corporate Debt: The Risk Structure of Interest Rates. *Journal of Finance* 29(2), 449–470.

Modigliani, F., and M. Miller. 1958. "The Cost of Capital, Corporation Finance and the Theory of Investment." *American Economic Review* 48, 267–297.

Modigliani, F., and M. Miller. 1963. "Corporate Income Taxes and the Cost of Capital: A Correction." *American Economic Review* 53(3), 433–443.

Musiela, M., and M. Rutkowski. 2005. *Martingale Methods in Financial Modeling.* New York: Springer-Verlag.

Rebonato, R. 2002. *Modern Pricing of Interest-Rate Derivatives: The LIBOR Market Model and Beyond.* Princeton, NJ: Princeton University Press.

Schönbucher, P. 2003. *Credit Derivatives Pricing Models: Model, Pricing and Implementation.* Hoboken, NJ: John Wiley & Sons.

INDEX